POLL BOOKS & ELECTION
RECORDS

2. The Midlands and Northern England

Jeremy Gibson and Colin Rogers

SECOND EDITION

Federation of Family History Societies

First published 1993 by the
Federation of Family History Societies.

Second edition, 1997, published by
Federation of Family History Societies (Publications) Ltd., c/o The Benson Room,
Birmingham and Midland Institute, Margaret Street, Birmingham B3 3BS, England.

Note. This second edition includes Worcestershire, which is duplicated in Part 3.

ISBN 1 86006 039 0

Computer typesetting in Arial, layout and cartography by Jeremy Gibson.
Cover graphics by Linda Haywood.
Cover illustration: from George Cruickshank's 'Oliver asking for more', in Charles
Dickens' *Oliver Twist*.

Printed by Parchment (Oxford) Limited.

Acknowedgements
Once again our deepest gratitude goes to the archivists who have responded so
conscientiously to yet another questionnaire, especially as this one was about
records often voluminous and not fully catalogued. In more than one record office
the response has been to spend time and energy on preparing such catalogues, and
we hope these will prove as useful on the spot as they have to us.
   A precursor of this national Guide was published in 1992 by the West Surrey
Family History Society, in *London, Middlesex and Surrey Workhouse Records: A
Guide to their nature and location*, by Cliff Webb (Research Aids **31**). With Cliff
Webb's collaboration the sections on these counties and the Metropolis are based
on this publication.
   Amongst individuals we would like to thank Simon Fowler at the Public Record
Office and Colin Harris at the Bodleian Library; Professor Michael E. Rose for
reading our Introduction; Stella Colwell for allowing us to reprint much of her succinct
description of PLU records from her admirable *Dictionary of Genealogical Sources in
the Public Record Office*; and John Blight for lending, for far longer than longer than
he had expected, the atlas to the 1845 edition of Lewis's *Topographical Dictionary of
England*.

                                                                    J.S.W.G., C.D.R.

Federation of Family History Societies (Publications) Ltd. is a wholly owned subsidiary of the Federation
of Family History Societies, Registered Charity No. 1038721.

CONTENTS

INTRODUCTION

The Old Poor Law

Poor Law Unions were the invention of the late seventeenth century. The Poor Law Acts of 1597 and 1601, and the Act of Settlement of 1662, had placed the responsibility for poor relief firmly in the hands of each parish, whose unpaid overseers of the poor had to collect rates from occupiers of land and property, and spend income on helping the destitute, apprenticing their children, setting the unemployed able bodied to work, and if necessary having them conveyed back to their own parish of settlement. The absence of a national poor rate was one of the factors which determined the shape of poor law policy until well into the twentieth century.

This reliance on the parish as the administrative unit was first seen to have its limitations in the towns whose economic unity contrasted sharply with the numerous closely adjoining parishes within them, and in 1696 Bristol was allowed by Act of Parliament to have a joint Union workhouse, for its nineteen parishes. The advantages of the workhouse system – entry therein could replace the offer of external or 'outdoor' relief, so it became the workhouse or nothing for the destitute – was soon realised by other places; Unions were established in a number of towns across the south of England during the next quarter of a century (listed in S. and D. Webb, 1927/1963, pp. 120-1) and Knatchbull's Act of 1723, allowing individual parishes to hire premises for the same purpose, did not prevent others from following suit.

Over time, however, workhouses proved to be expensive – more so than giving outdoor relief, and Gilbert's Act of 1782 allowed Unions (each under a Board of Guardians) to give such relief to the able bodied while retaining workhouse places for the aged and infirm. Further liberalisation followed – from 1795, no one was to be removed under the Settlement Laws unless they were healthy, and had applied for relief, and support could be given even to those refusing admission to a workhouse. The Speenhamland system of 1795, recognising a sliding scale for outdoor relief which related to the price of grain, was only one such device by which individual parishes or Unions recognised the need to relate the level of financial assistance to the prevailing economic circumstances. Some relief was given in the shape of assisted passage for emigrants.

There were several problems for the development or even continuation of this system. The desire to offer outdoor relief in exchange for work directed by the poor law authority was thwarted by a lack of opportunity for such labour; some recipients were seen to be paid for being idle, and employers were believed to pay deliberately low wages, knowing that the balance of a living wage would be made up by the parish or Union. A significant number of the poor, particularly immigrants, were unassisted because of the Settlement Laws; on the other hand, in the eyes of many employers and economists, too many potential labourers were being removed from a free market. Expenditure on poor relief was perceived to be out of control, being related to demand rather than supply.

The New Poor Law of 1834

It seems a singular irony that the reforming Whig government of the 1830's should have introduced a piece of legislation which, even at the time, seemed one of the most draconian in our modern history. The paradox is one between the intent and the effect of 1834, not between 1834 and other measures. The enemy was not seen as poverty (which was merely a shortage of money, an ineradicable feature of a stratified society), but pauperism, a character defect involving idleness, unreliability, drunkenness etc., which led so many of its victims into desperate financial straits, and threatened the stability, if not the fabric, of society. Paupers were encouraged to breed by the very financial support which had been given in outdoor relief for the previous half century, and it was this belief, coupled with the ever increasing demands on ratepayers, which led the new government to set up a Royal Commission in 1832, on whose report the New Poor Law was based.

The Commission devised a simple way to eradicate pauperism at minimum cost and bureaucratic intervention – the system itself, an institutional stimulus-response experiment in utilitarianism, would compel the indigent to reform in order to avoid conditions in the workhouse which were to be deliberately worse than that of an 'independent labourer of the lowest class', a principle known as 'less eligibility'. Outdoor relief was to be phased out within two years, and paupers accepting indoor relief were to be made to feel like unwelcome guests.

The Act of 1834 implementing these recommendations was to be enforced by a national Commission which was to compel the formation of Poor Law Unions, each the responsibility of a Board of Guardians (partly ex-officio and partly elected by ratepayers). The Board appointed permanent officers, principally the relieving officer and workhouse master, supervised the activities of those officers, and spent the poor rates, normally through a committee structure. This included removal under the Settlement Laws (some 15,000 p.a. still being removed up the First World War), or paying other Unions to maintain 'their' paupers. The rates were still estimated according to the demands on each parish until 1865, when a Union rate replaced them. The Guardians remained until 1930; the Commission became the Poor Law Board in 1847, the Local Government Board in 1871, and was part of the Ministry of Health from 1919.

There was, of course, considerable resistance to the new scheme, whose workhouses were often referred to as 'bastilles'; in some parts of the industrial north, indeed, the very creation of Boards of Guardians was delayed for years, and even then, the intention of 1834 was subverted by Guardians unwilling to implement it (see Cole, 1984, Introduction). The extent of the effectiveness of the anti-Poor Law movement, however, has been questioned by Karel Williams (1981) who asserts that in those areas, outdoor relief to able bodied male adults was cut, being available from 1842 only as a reward for unpleasant tasks assigned by the Guardians, leaving an increasing number with no assistance at all. It certainly seems to be the case that this class, for whom 1834 was really intended, never formed anything like a majority of those being granted indoor relief. By the 1860's, all Unions had workhouses, usually of the 'general' kind in which all inmates were housed, regardless of age, sex, or reason for being there.

In addition to a hostile public opinion, the Victorian Guardians had to face recurrent problems over which they had little control. Unemployment in the cotton industry during the so-called 'cotton famine' (1862-65) was closely followed by the 'Lancet' scandal of 1865 which revealed the dreadful state of some of the medical wards in workhouses as dirty and poorly managed. Increasing criticism from socialists (through the Fabian Society) and others culminated in the famous published surveys by Charles Booth in London (from 1889) and Rowntree in York (1901) which demonstrated the true causes of poverty as unemployment, underemployment, the death of a wage earner in the family, or having large numbers of children – indigence as a character trait did not even appear as a category. The gradual enfranchisement of the working classes gave opponents of the system a stronger political foothold, and from 1894 the property qualification to become a member of a Board of Guardians was abolished.

The weakness of the 'pauperism' theory underlying the New Poor Law had been recognised by the Charity Organisation Society, founded in 1869, which divided the poor into 'deserving' (who should be treated by charitable organisations) and 'undeserving', for whom the poor law was designed. After 1871, there was an increasing specialisation in Union institutions, recognising that the 'general' workhouse could not adequately cater for those whose circumstances were radically different from each other -- the infirm, the aged, the sick, the children, the lunatics, and the unemployed. Children, for example, were raised in cottage homes in many Unions. The amount spent on out relief fell as this specialisation increased.

With hindsight, it seems astonishing that the New Poor Law should have survived well into the twentieth century, and can only be understood if it is recognised that its functions became increasingly vestigial as the years went by. From 1834, it might be viewed as a catch-all welfare system in which the Guardians had to treat all those who could not maintain themselves, and, because of this breadth of clientele, the Guardians were given responsibilities seemingly removed from the Poor Law itself. From 1836, for example, they had to oversee civil registration, and from 1850, sanitation and vaccination. From 1877, in areas without a School Board, they oversaw school attendance; and, from 1897 outside London, infant life protection. They housed youngsters in detention following the 1908 Children Act. Often, Union infirmaries dealt with cases from the population at large, especially during the First World War.

However, the growing conviction that functionalism – i.e., that different functions of welfare should be the responsibility of different agencies – was more effective led to the successive withdrawal of these functions from the Guardians. London hospitals took over in 1867; the School Boards and, later, County and Borough Councils gradually gained responsibility for the education of all children after 1870. Unemployment began to be countered by labour exchanges from 1909, and insurance rather than the workhouse from 1911. The Old Age Pension was introduced in 1908, and health insurance in 1911. There was, however, always something left for the Guardians to do.

Given these changes, both Majority and Minority reports of the Royal Commission on the Poor Laws, 1905-1909, advocated the abolition of the Guardians, and the virtual full employment during the First World War meant that they were becoming 'increasingly irrelevant'. However, the tidal wave of unemployment in the early 1920's ensured a continuing role, albeit as a backstop to the new insurance schemes which quickly spent the surplus which had accumulated during the war. Neither the Guardians nor the state had an adequate answer to unemployment on such a scale, and the 643 Boards of Guardians were abolished on 1 April 1930, though the Poor Law itself, including the Act of Settlement, lingered on until 1948.

The Records

We know of no single guide describing the contents of all the Union records, and it is clear that titles as well as contents might vary somewhat with time and place.

Union Records in the Public Record Office

As the main class of interest, **MH 12**, consists of 16,741 volumes (most of 500 to 1,000 pages) arranged by county (alphabetically) and within each county, by Union (alphabetically), the description, with precise references under each Union, is confined to 'Corres. etc. 1834-1900'. In the case of many Unions, this must be the major (sometimes only) nineteenth century source. It is certain to include names of countless individuals and some lists (for instance for sponsored emigration of paupers), particularly for the earlier decades.

MH 12 is described by Stella Colwell in her *Dictionary of Genealogical Sources* (page 52) as follows:

'Correspondence from the Boards and local authorities with the Poor Law Commission to 1847, and its successor, the Poor Law Board, and papers including applications for posts as Relieving Officer, schoolteacher, chaplain, medical officer, master and matron of the workhouse, embracing curriculum vitae, testimonials from previous employers or friends, letters of appointment, resignation and dismissal, vaccination records, details of lunatic inmates, examinations of paupers seeking help, provision for emigration, and information on outbreaks of infectious diseases. Within each Union records are arranged chronologically.'

MH 12 is indexed by subject in **MH 15**. However, the entries are very specialised and give no names or localities, so the indexes are unlikely to be of any use to family or local historians.

Post-1900 correspondence is continued in **MH 68**, but many volumes were destroyed during the Second World War, and the references are not provided in this Guide.

The other class referenced here under individual Unions in **MH 9**. Its volumes (arranged by Unions, or London districts, in alphabetical order) contain details of staffing, listing every officer employed in whatever capacity, dates of appointment and departure (with reasons for leaving) and their salary. The paid officers of one typical Union, Banbury in Oxfordshire, at various times included clerk, treasurer, chaplain, medical officers, master, matron, schoolmaster and mistress, porter, nurse, assistant in vagrant wards, assistant matron or superintendent nurse, many assistant nurses, tailor, clerk to School Attendance Committee, school attendance officers, inquiry officers, medical and relieving officers (by place) and vaccination officers (by district). The class list suggests these cover from 1837 to 1921. In fact, some appointments date from as early as 1835, but many Unions do not appear to have had full-time staff before the 1850's or 1860's. The date of the earliest appointment can be misleading, as this may be that of part-time staff, such as clerk, chaplain, baker, schoolmaster or mistress. The overall dates are usually given under each Union, but the register must be consulted to discover when a staffed workhouse actually became established. Further staff appointments, 1834-50 (not referenced here), are in **MH 19**.

Other 'Poor Law' classes are described as follows:

MH 14: plans of land and buildings, listed alphabetically by Union, 1861-1918; **MH 19/22**: correspondence with Government Offices concerning emigration of the poor, 1837-76; **MH 64**: official sanction permitting expenditure on assisted emigration of the poor, and for casual vacancies on the Boards of Guardians, 1916-32; **MH 32**: correspondence of Assistant Poor Law Commissioners and Inspectors, arranged alphabetically by name and reporting on workhouse conditions, 1834-1904; **MH 33**: registers of MH 32 correspondence, 1834-46; **MH 27**: correspondence between Poor Law Boards and Poor Law School Districts for administration and control of schools, appointment of managers, teaching and nursing staff, 1848-1910; **MH 18**: Visiting Officers' diaries concerning Metropolitan Casual Wards of vagrants, some containing dates of death of officers, and applications for vacant posts, 1874-78, 1881.

Census returns of staff and inmates in Union workhouses will be found in the decennial censuses from 1841 on (available at present to 1891).

There is an excellent introduction to the series by K.M. Thompson (1987) The calendar of the **MH 12** series is published in List and Index Society *Ministry of Health Poor Law Union Papers* vols. **56**, *(Bedford - Kent)*, **64**, *(Lancashire - co. Southampton)*, **77**, *(Stafford - Yorkshire - Wales)*. This shows the years covered by individual volumes of the series for each Union, but provides no additional information to that given here.

Union records in County and other local Record Offices

The main records generated by the Unions themselves concerning their day to day operations, where they survive, are held locally. Records of the Poor Law Guardians are sometimes the most voluminous series in a record office, reflected in this, the most extensive in the 'Gibson Guides' series so far. They are of interest to a wide variety of historians, economic, social, and political. Their very size, and the order in which the items are contained, have made them difficult to use, and they are therefore among the most under-exploited of major sources still to be opened up for personal or historical investigation.

The fullest description appears to be that in the published handlist to the Somerset Poor Law records, which was, we understand, the first to devise a classification for this type of record, but which has been expanded and clarified in the classification which follows. Several other record offices have published guides to their collections, often including an introduction to the records themselves. We have not followed this classification order in the Guide itself, as it had been devised for archival, rather than historical, use. What we call category 'A' records, those with substantial numbers of names of the general public or inmates, are given below in **bold type**.

Clerk to the Guardians

Board and Officers: Lists of members; service registers, acceptances, standing orders, superannuation returns, declarations of office, attendance books.

Minutes: Board of Guardians (**occasionally with lists of inmates**), in later years sometimes printed;

Committees (e.g. finance, (work)house, boarding-out (**sometimes with lists of children**), relief etc.

Accounts (uniform nationally from 1848): Annual or half-yearly accounts were sometimes printed, and may include **names of those relieved**;

Ledgers (general, treasurer's, parochial (till 1927), non-settled and non-resident poor (from 1845 only));

Petty cash;

Returns of paupers relieved (quarterly);

Financial statements (some statutory);

Precepts for, and statements of expenditure (incl. out of loans);

Poor rate returns;

Claims for grants in aid of poor rate expenditure (agricultural land, maintenance of pauper lunatics, repayment of salaries of teachers in poor law schools, and medical officers);

Loans granted to paupers (incl. name, parish, cause of loan, date, length, repayment);

Maintenance of indoor paupers in institutions of other authorities.

Lunacy: Maintenance;
Statements of conditions;
Registers of clothing;
Register of lunatics in asylums;
List of lunatics not in asylums;
Return of pauper lunatics (from 1842, name, age, sex, where maintained, and cost).
Statistics: Returns (weekly, fortnightly, monthly, half-yearly and annual; **weekly can include names**);
Miscellaneous returns, incl. pauper children;
Pauper classification book.
Case Papers: **Case papers on each person relieved, incl. dependents**.

Out-relief

Relief order book (applicant, parish, amount and period);
Register of non-resident and non-settled poor (name, residence, Union amount etc.);
Register of relief granted on loan;
Report of relief granted to aliens (1914-20);
Receipts of rent of pay stations.
Workhouses and Children's Homes: Buildings and provision documents (maps, supplies, contracts).
Supplies: Tenders.
Mortgages: Register of mortgages for loans on security of rates.
Children: **Register of children under control of the Guardians** (from 1889);
Indentures of apprenticeship of pauper children (from 1844);
Register of apprentices (from 1844) **and children placed in service** (from 1851);
Records of children apprenticed or employed;
Register of children boarded-out;
Reports by boarding-out visitors;
Accounts of maintenance of boarded-out children;
Miscellaneous files relating to boarding-out.
Irremovability, Settlement and Removal: Reports of removable and irremovable poor;
Settlement journey book;
Records of examination on application for removal orders;
Orders of adjudication and removal;
Consent to receive paupers without justices' order.
Recovery of relief: **Agreements by relatives to contribute**;
Orders for contributions by relatives.

Appointment of overseers: Appointment documents.
Statements received for preservation:
Overseers' balance sheets;
Rate collectors' monthly statements;
Orders for maintenance under the Bastardy Act 1845.
Miscellaneous: **List of paupers**;
Correspondence.

Treasurer

Treasurer's books and accounts.

Workhouse Master

Regulations: Regulations for the conduct of institution and staff;
Admission and discharge book (names, dates, occupation, age, religion, parish, cause of need of relief, class of diet; occasionally indexed, with full list of inmates, parish of settlement etc.);
Register of admission without orders;
Register of admission and discharge to workhouse school;
Register of admission refused;
Register of births in the workhouse (baptismal name, date of birth, sex, name(s) of parents, from what parish admitted, when and where baptised);
Register of baptisms in the workhouse,
Register of deaths in the workhouse (name, age, date of death, from what parish admitted, where buried);
Register of burials;
Register of sickness and mortality;
Register of apprentices and servants placed from the workhouse (date, master's name, trade and residence; sometimes age and parents);
Indoor relief list (name, date of birth, 'calling', creed, number of days in the workhouse; sometimes indexed; compiled every six months from admission and discharge books);
Medical examination books (inmates, children, alleged lunatics);
Workhouse medical relief book (name, age, date in sick ward, diet, when discharged etc.);
Records of lunatics in workhouse (register, detention certificates, register of mechanical restraint, notice to coroner of deaths, post-mortem books);
Medical Officer's reports on mental or bodily disease (lists and general reports);

Register of inmates;

Creed register (from 1876; name, date of birth, date and place of admission, creed, source of information, date of discharge or death; some give occupation, last address, name and address of nearest relative);

Individual record cards;

Leave of absence book;

Labour book;

Loans to paupers (mainly to pay for funerals);

Certificates of employment of pauper nurses and of inmates in sick wards;

Register of inmates' own clothing;

Register of applications and complaints by inmates;

Bathing register;

[Offences and] punishment book (name, date, offence, punishment by Master and Guardians);

Register of addresses of paupers' next of kin and friends;

Notices of illness or death to next of kin or friends.

Reports: Porter's book (**sometimes lists visitors and reasons for visits**);

Porter's admission and discharge book;

Report books of chaplain, matron, nurse, fire brigade;

Master's report book or journal (from 1842);

Report books of various visiting committees: general, lunatics, children, ladies etc.

Accounts: Master's day book;

Master's receipt and payment book;

Salaries and wages receipt book;

Officers' allowance account;

Workhouse minor accounts: baking, farm, garden, pig, oakum, stone, wood, bedding, crockery, linen, coffin, provisions, 'necessaries' and miscellaneous (tobacco, snuff etc.), heating, lighting, cleaning, clothing;

Order/requisition books;

Inventory books;

Dietaries (general, children's etc. by class);

Drug stock book.

Relief to casual poor: **Register of wayfarers received;**

Admission and discharge of casuals (date, hour, names of family, age, occupation, where slept previous night, cash in hand, work done during stay, where going next);

Records of ex-servicemen passing through casual wards;

Dietary table for casual poor.

Miscellaneous: Correspondence;

Receipts and expenses for workhouse.

Officer in charge of children's home

Indoor relief list;

Admission and discharge book;

Superintendent's report book;

Visitor's report book;

Inventory;

Provisions and necessaries accounts.

Relieving officer

Out relief lists (1834-47, with abstracts);

Out relief book (or **relief order books** 1848-1911; name, number, address, amount of relief, period);

Relief order lists (1911-30);

Abstracts of application and report (1834-47);

Application and report book (from 1847; name, age, date, address, length of stay, occupation, marital status; if a child, orphaned/deserted/illegitimate; if disabled, whether seeking medical relief, cause for seeking relief, date of visits to pauper's address, amount of relief ordered; some early ones might give place of settlement, ages of wife and children, names of relations liable for help, how long resident);

Receipt and expenditure book (from 1847; surnames only);

Diaries;

Orders for medical relief;

Pauper description book/list (names of applicant and family, address, year(s) of birth, disability, marital status, occupation, place of settlement, date first chargeable, present cause of relief, names and occupations of dependents);

Orders on tradesmen for relief in kind;

Out-relief lists of vagrants;

Relief to aliens' wives (1914-19; name of wife, address, number of children, amount given);

Miscellaneous forms and reports;

Register of visits to young persons under 16 hired or taken as servants from workhouse (name, age, date of hire, name and residence of master/mistress, trade, date of present and previous visits, whether servant was satisfied by position).

District Medical Officer
DMO relief book/list (name, age, parish, disease/accident, diet, treatment, fitness for employment);
DMO report book.

Collector of the Guardians
Collector's ledger;
Statement of arrears;
Receipt and payment book.

Non-poor law statutory duties
Civil registration: Returns of births and deaths;
Marriage notice books;
List of buildings registered for marriage;
Census plans etc.;
Correspondence;
Census register of children (name, residence, date of birth, present and previous school if any).
*Vaccination:*Vaccination committee minute books;
Vaccination registers;
Vaccinators' registers (name, date and place of birth, sex, name of father (or mother if illegitimate), father's occupation, when registered, date and recipient of vaccinator's notice, date of successful vaccination, or 'insusceptability');
Vaccination officer's report book;
Returns to central authority;
Contracts with public vaccinators;
Prosecution papers (from 1867).
Assessment: Assessment committee books;
Rate books;
Valuation books/lists (usually address, value, owner and tenant);
Returns of assessable values;
Correspondence, appeals etc.

Sanitation: Inspector of Nuisances report book;
Rural Sanitary Authority minute books (from 1872);
Allotments Committee books;
Bye-laws;
Ledgers, incl. parochial;
Clerk's petty cash book;
Medical Officer's reports;
Receipt and expenditure returns;
Register of common lodging houses;
Correspondence and miscellaneous.
School attendance: School Attendance Committee minute books (1877-1903);
Register of exemption certificates;
School Attendance Officer's reports;
Medical Officer's reports on school children;
School fees application and report book (name, date, age, relationship of applicant to child, number and ages of children under 16, applicant's age, address, occupation, marital status, if disabled, weekly earnings, name of school, length there, fee, and period ordered);
School fees order book;
School fees receipt and payment book;
Correspondence and miscellaneous.
Infant life protection: **Register of persons receiving infants**;
Register of infants received,
Inspector's reports on infants;
Notices to Guardians from persons retaining or receiving infants;
Notices to Guardians of removal of infant from care.

PRESENTATION

The following general points should be noted.

Whether or not closure is specifically mentioned in the text of the guide, it should be assumed that individual medical records are likely to be inaccessible to the public until they are one hundred years old. In many repositories records of individuals - just those of the greatest interest to family historians - are arbitrarily closed for any time up to a hundred years from the date of the last entry. This contrasts with the occasional printed reports which may include lists of paupers relieved, information that the Guardians of the time considered public property!

Bearing in mind the majority readership of the Gibson Guides, we have attempted to present records in two groups. Group **A** (in bold in the foregoing list) are those records which contain large numbers of names of the public at the time, usually because they were in the workhouse or had applied for outside relief. Group **B** are therefore the rest, often including the names and details of those who worked for the Unions concerned.

Descriptions of records by title vary from one Union to another, and it is possible that, occasionally, one will be entered under the wrong category (**A** or **B**). We apologise in advance, and hope that users of the records will be able to alert the editors to such discrepancies.

Because of the pressure of space, we have not been able to include the reference numbers of the records themselves (except those in the Public Record Office) and hope that record offices are not unduly inconvenienced by this. We have, for the same reason, excluded those records (such as copies of Acts of Parliament) which could be easily obtained elsewhere, and records which pertain only to one event or individual.

'Gaps' should be taken to mean that not all years are available between the dates stated

'Part' implies that the record is not available for the whole of the Union

'Various' indicates that there are both gaps in the series, and also that the whole Union is not covered.

Numerous abbreviations have been used throughout the Guide. They are listed inside the front cover.

Further reading and references

A. Benton, 'Sponsored migration under the New Poor Law', *Oxfordshire Family Historian* **2**.9 (1982) and *Midland Ancestor* **6**.8 (1983).

J. Cole, *Down poorhouse lane: the diary of a Rochdale workhouse* (Introduction) (1984).

J.A. Coleman, 'Guardians' minute books'. *History* **48** (1963).

S. Colwell, *Dictionary of genealogical sources in the Public Record Office* (1992).

M.A. Crowther, *The Workhouse system, 1834-1929* (1981).

A. Digby, *The poor law in nineteenth century England and Wales* (1982).

A. Digby, *Pauper palaces* (1978) (with special reference to Norfolk).

S. Fowler, *Assistant Poor Law Commissioners' Correspondence* (Short Guides to Records, Historical Association, 1995).

D. Fraser, *The new poor law in the nineteenth century* (1976).

P. Harling, 'The power of persuasion: central authority, local bureaucracy and the New Poor Law', *English Historical Review* **107** (1992).

N. Longmate, *The workhouse* (1974).

P. Mandler, 'Tories and paupers: Christian political economy and the making of the New Poor Law', *The Historical Journal* **33** (1990).

P. Mandler, 'The making of the New Poor Law *redivivus*', *Past and Present* (1987).

R. Noschke and R. Rocker, 'Civilian internment in Britain during the first world war', *Anglo-German Family History Society* (1989).

A. Reid, *The Union Workhouse: a study guide for teachers and local historians*, BALH 'Learning Local History **3**' (1994).

P. Riden, *Record sources for local history* (1987) (pp 112-117).

M.E. Rose, *The English poor law 1780-1930* (1971).

M.E. Rose, *The relief of poverty 1834-1914* (1972, 1986).

M.E. Rose, *The poor and the city: the English poor law in its urban context, 1834-1914* (1985).

W.B. Stephens, *Sources for English local history* (2nd edition, 1981).

K.M. Thompson, 'Sources for the New Poor Law in the public records', *Journal of Regional and Local Studies* **7**.1 (1987).

R. Vorspan, 'Vagrancy and the New Poor Law in late-Victorian and Edwardian England', *English Historical Review* **92** (1977).

S. and B. Webb, *English poor law policy* (1910/1963).

S. and B. Webb, *English poor law history: part 1 - the old poor law* (1929); *part 2 - the last hundred years* (1929).

K. Williams, *From pauperism to poverty* (1981).

P. Wood, *Poverty and the workhouse in Victorian Britain* (1991).

MAPS

The figures in square brackets after each Union heading identify their location on the county maps. These are based on the maps in the 1845 edition of Lewis's *Topographical Dictionary of England* and the companion work on *Wales*. Although most of the country was already unionised, there were, as mentioned in the Introduction, places which still resisted this requirement. In most counties it has been possible to identify such areas with the Unions they eventually became. The only major area to defy such identification is a large swathe of the West Riding of Yorkshire, where it has been necessary to leave the boundaries of the many eventual Unions of this populous area undefined. It must be borne in mind that after 1845 further Unions were created out of existing ones, or boundaries changed. The maps are there to give an idea of the geographical location of Unions (and civil registration and census districts), especially those overlapping county borders, but, even for 1845, are not guaranteed as accurate.

The places which made up each English Union at any time are shown in the Gazetteer which is part 4 of this Guide, based on information given in F.A. Youngs, jr., *Local Administrative Units in England* (Royal Historical Society, 1981, 1991). The Gazetteer also shows the places constituting each Union in Wales (including Monmouthshire) at the time of the 1851 census.

CHESHIRE

See T. Benton, "'Here is a living and a good one.'" Movement to Lancashire and Cheshire under the 1835-7 Sponsored Poor Law Migration scheme', *Lancashire* (Lancashire F.H.S.) **7**.1 (Feb. 1986).

Unless shown otherwise, records are at **Cheshire Record Office,** *Chester.*
See Caroline M. Williams, *Guide to the Cheshire Record Office*, Cheshire C.C., 1991, pp. 37-39.
Prior notice is required, as the records are stored elsewhere.

Altrincham [5] (Bucklow from 1890s).
A. Reg. of settlement cases 1911-30; reg. of lunatics 1903-10; reg. of orphaned children boarded-out 1869-1923; out relief order books 1928-34; consent to receive paupers without JP's order 1915-29; deaths reg. 1898-1940; reg. of persons receiving infants for reward 1919-26; indexed reg. of inmates 1908-40; reg. of mechanical restraint 1907-39; inmates' case files 1922-40 (restricted access); reg. of non-settled cases 1927-36; valuation lists (various) between 1904 and 1939.
B. Min's 1844-48, 1865-74, 1877-86, 1888-1928; C'tee min's. Assessment 1862-1950, Finance 1908-1928, Children's and Homes 1915-20, Relief 1928-1937, SAC 1887-95 (damaged) with bye laws 1878-1880, RSA 1872-78, 1882-94; PLC orders 1836; Guardians' attendance reg's 1896-1930; reg. of salaries and deductions 1899-1922; ledger 1839-1840, 1850-52, 1889-90, 1895-1928; treasurer's ledger 1907-29; parochial ledger 1902-30; financial statements 1920-30; reg. of repayment by relatives 1893-1936 (part); returns of numbers chargeable, weekly 1927-32, half-yearly 1923-30 (gaps); overseers' balance sheets 1908-27, letter book 1912-13; treasurer's receipt and exp. books 1919-1925; master's report books 1920-55; inventories 1907-40.
Public Record Office, Kew:
Corres. etc. 1834-1900 [MH 12/770-811]; staff reg. 1837-1921 [MH 9/1 (Altrincham), MH 9/3 (Bucklow)].

Ashton-under-Lyne [7] (Dukinfield, Godley, Hattersley, Hollingworth, Matley, Newton, Mottram, Stalybridge, Stayley, Tintwistle).
See under Lancashire.

Birkenhead (PLU formed in 1861).
Birkenhead Central Library:
A. Reg. of children sent to institutions and service etc. 1904-09; persons sent to institutions and service 1909-24; list of applicants not chargeable 1907-10; persons chargeable at Infirmary c.1918-30 (alphabetical); visitors' reports on persons maintained in other institutions 1925-42; affiliation orders 1928-38; creed reg. 1869-1950;

schools adm. and discharge reg's 1889-98; births reg's 1864-1914; baptisms reg's 1890-1950; deaths reg's 1864-1944; reg's of inmates' property 1897-1956; Infirmary: creed reg's 1913-37, births reg's 1913-42, deaths reg's 1913-36; marriage notice books 1907-17; valuation lists 1863-69 (Bidston-cum-Fird 1887-1920, Birkenhead 1871-1929, Claughton-cum-Grange 1884-97, Liscard 1870-1912, Noctorum 1884-1914, Oxton 1871-97, Poulton-cum-Seacombe 1872-1912, Tranmere 1870-97, Wallasey 1884-1920).
B. Min's 1861-1930 (printed from 1909); attendance reg's 1907-30; agenda books 1906-08, 1916-22; c'tee min's: General 1861-69, Boarding-out 1910-13, Central Relief 1920-24, Children's Home and Sanatorium 1900-13, Finance 1887-1930, Hospital and Infirmary 1900-04, Infirmary 1913, SAC 1887-94, Schools 1887-98, Special 1912-29, Work for Unemployed Persons 1928, W'h. and Schools Visiting 1871-86, W'h. 1887-1913; corres. 1861-1914; out letters 1914-40; PLB/LGB letters 1861-1930; reg's of appointments 1919-30, salaries 1913-1928, sup'an. 1897-1920; leave of absence book 1893-1935; press cuttings 1913-32; tenders etc. re. offices 1901-05; stat. statements 1867-82; financial state-ments 1861-1901; ledgers 1861-1930; parochial ledgers 1861-1927, reg's of rents payable c.1910-c.1924; bank book 1928-30; children's dinner ac's 1884-5; w'h. wages ac's 1922-42; Children's Homes' Superintendent out letters 1905-17; maps and plans (n.d., c.1860's?); hospital wages 1922-42; reg. of probationers' training 1899-1921.
Public Record Office, Kew:
Corres. etc. 1861-1900 [MH 12/821-61]; staff reg. 1837-1921 [MH 9/2].

Boughton, Great [3] (from 1871 **Tarvin**).
B. Min's 1837-1929; ledger 1862-1927; Assessment C'tee min's 1862-1927; RSA general ledger 1878-90, parochial ledger 1886-88.
Chester City Record Office.
A. Assessment and collection of rates 1891-1929 (as Tarvin).
Public Record Office, Kew:
Corres. etc. 1835-1900 [MH.12/877-98]; staff reg. 1837-1921 [MH 9/3 (Gt. Boughton), MH 9/17 (Tarvin)].

Bucklow - see Altrincham

Chester [2] (Incorporation 1762-1869, PLU from 1869) (partly Flints.).
Chester City Record Office:
A. Reg's and lists of inmates 1875-1954; births reg. 1914-43; reg. of burials and graves in Union cemetery 1882-1900; assessment and collection of rates 1909-29 (also some parish collections: Chester 1885-1928, Hale 1880-1928, Bache 1863-1897, Caughall 1863-97, Newton by Chester 1867-1898, Upton by Chester 1867-9?)

B. Ac's 1913-33; orders etc. re. w'h. building 1872-1931; w'h. plans 1878-1930.
Public Record Office, Kew:
Corres. etc. 1834-1900 [MH 12/900-27]; staff reg. 1837-1921 [MH 9/4].

Congleton [11] (partly in Staffs.).
See *At the Crossroads: A History of Arclid Workhouse and Hospital,* by Marlene and Grham Langley, 1993. £4,95 from the authors, 37 The Fairway, Alsager, Stoke-on-Trent, ST7 2BD.
A. Reg. of inmates c.1901-56; births reg. 1914-49; baptisms reg. 1902-51; deaths reg. 1837-1963; creed reg. 1901-48.
B. Min's 1837-1930; Poor Relief C'tee min's 1895-1917; inventory books 1901-25, 1929-50; ledgers 1850-1923; parochial ledgers 1859-1910; vac. officer's report books 1922-43.
Public Record Office, Kew:
Corres. etc. 1834-1900 [MH 12/934-62]; staff reg. 1837-1921 [MH 9/5].

Drayton, Market [14] (Tittenley).
See under Shropshire.

Hawarden (Claverton, Dodleston, Eaton, Eccleston, Lower Kinnerton, Marlston cum Lache, Poulton, Pulford, Gt. and Lit. Saughall, Shotwick, Woodbank, until 1871).
See under Wales: Flintshire.

Hayfield [8] (Disley).
See under Derbyshire.

Macclesfield [10].
A. Adm. and discharge reg's 1863-1940; children's adm. and discharge reg's 1913-33 (in alphabetical order until 1916); inmates' reg's 1896-1940 (alphabetical order); military patients' adm. and discharge reg's 1914-25; reg. of mechanical restraint 1895-1934; births reg. 1848-65; baptisms reg. 1898-1930; deaths reg. 1848-1949; creed reg. 1885-90, 1902-23; punishment book 1849-1912.
B. Conveyances and mortgages 1843-1904; c'tee min's 1880-1922; reg'ns for casual paupers c.1871; typescript article re. history and present condition of w'h. c.1880.
Macclesfield Library:
'Reports received by the PLC in 1841 on the state of the Macclesfield and Bolton Unions'; G.A. Oliver, 'The process of PL reform in the Macclesfield Union 1834-1845', B.Ed. thesis, 1981.
Public Record Office, Kew:
Corres. etc. 1834-1900 [MH 12/968-1005]; staff reg. 1837-1921 [MH 9/11].

Market Drayton [14] (Tittenley).
See under Shropshire.

Nantwich [13] (* = restricted access).
A. Reg. of inmates c.1925-49; *removal orders and related papers 1894-1930; births/vac's reg.: Bunbury 1906-10, Wrenbury 1872-1909; *lists of children with no vac. cert's 1908-9; LGB memos re. smallpox 1901 and revac. 1902.
B. Min's 1842-56, 1858-70, 1872-83, 1885-99, 1901-13, 1915-17, 1923-30; ledger 1922-25; parochial ledger 1838-76; Finance C'tee min's 1891-1920 (with *loose papers); *Building C'tee reports 1894-1912; parochial ledger 1908-27; *staff appointments, salaries etc. 1896-1930; *corres. re. relief work and unemployment 1922; statement re. out relief 1929; *corres. with other PLUs 1899-1926; *assessment returns 1894-1926; annual ac's 1892-97.
Public Record Office, Kew:
Corres. etc. 1834-1900 [MH 12/1013-50]; staff reg. 1837-1921 [MH 9/12].

Northwich [9].
A. Births reg. 1849-1913; deaths reg. 1855-1914; reg. of inmates 1919-46; creed reg's 1872-1942; alphabetical list of persons aged 65 and over 1923-1942.
B. Min's 1883-86, 1920-25; ledgers 1836-1929; treasurer's ledgers 1905-24; parochial ledgers 1848-1927; non-settled and non-resident poor ledgers 1845-48; domestic ac's, Weaver Hall, some from 1918-1930+.
Public Record Office, Kew:
Corres. etc. 1834-1900 [MH 12/1059-95]; staff reg. 1837-1921 [MH 9/12].

Runcorn [4].
A. Vac. reg's: Frodsham 1871-1931, Budworth 1928-48.
B. Summary of proceedings of vac. officer 1915-1948.
Public Record Office, Kew:
Corres. etc. 1836-1900 [MH 12/1103-30]; staff reg. 1837-1921 [MH 9/14].

Stockport [6] (partly Lancs.).
Most PLU records are believed to have been destroyed during World War II).
Stockport Central Library:
A. Lists of inmates and removals 1841-43; contributions towards upkeep of inmates 1833-57; lists of paupers 1837-43, 1853-73 (gaps); list of lunatics 1883; annual return of lunatics 1913; rate books 1808-1924 (arrears 1830, 1845-47; summonses 1850-57,1907-13); settlement books 1830-38); vac. reg's 1871-1902 (missing 1900); valuation lists 1844-1922 (gaps); MO's order book 1840; reg. of deaths and diseases 1874-95; reg's of infectious diseases cert's and of medical practitioners 1890-1913; Assessment C'tee list of objections etc. 1843-1915; list of scholarship students 1891.

B. C'tee min's: Boarding-out and Children's 1896-1915, 1917-28, Finance 1899-1927 (missing 1923), Misc. 1896-1915, 1922-29, Stepping Hill Hospital 1906-29 (with reg'ns 1906), Stones 1906-16, 1918-28, W'h. and General Purposes 1900-29; SAC 1882-1913; Technical Instruction 1891-1909; PLC orders forming the PLU 1838; PLB and LGB corres. 1834-1900; MoH's report books 1882-1904 and stat's 1908-13; collectors' statements 1848-1920; abstract of ac's 1850-1, 1853-4, 1895; balance sheets 1860-69; ac's (fragments) 1887-92; estimate for new offices 1905; Year Books 1902/3, 1911/2, 1913/4.

Public Record Office, Kew:
Corres. etc. 1834-1899 [MH 12/1138-82]; staff reg. 1837-1921 [MH 9/16].

Tarvin see **Boughton, Great**.

Warrington (Grappenhall, Latchford, Thelwall).
See under Lancashire.

Wem (Whitchurch).
See under Shropshire.

Whitchurch (from 1853; asterisked places were in Wrexham PLU until 1853: *Agden, *Bickley, *Bradley, *Chidlow, *Chorlton, *Cuddington, Duckington, Edge, Hampton, Larkton, Macefen, *Malpas, Marbury with Quoisley, *Newton by Malpas, *Norbury, *Oldcastle, *Overton, *Stockton, Threapwood (from 1894), Tushingham cum Grindley, *Wigland, Wirswall, *Wychough).
See under Shropshire.

Wirral [1].
B. Min's 1836-91 (gaps); C'tee min's: W'h. 1892-1926 (gaps), Boarding-out 1910-26, Infirmary 1915-26, General Purpose 1922-26, Children's 1925-6, SAC 1883-94; treasurer's ac's 1906-25; master's report books, Clatterbridge Hospital, 1924-33; visitors' report books 1918-48; chaplain's report book 1912-31; misc.: PLC orders, w'h. building, rules 1836-42.

Chester City Record Office:
A. Assessment and collection of rates 1909-28.
Public Record Office, Kew:
Corres. etc. 1834-1900 [MH 12/1200-31]; staff reg. 1837-1921 [MH 9/19].

Wrexham [12] (Church Shocklach, Shocklach Oviatt; until 1853, places later in Whitchurch PLU, as asterisked above; also Threapwood).
See under Wales: Denbighshire.

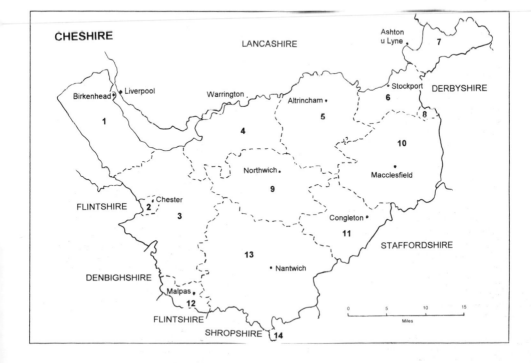

CUMBERLAND

See R.N. Thompson, 'The working of the Poor Law Amendment Act in Cumbria 1836-1871', *Northern History* **15** (1979).

Except when shown otherwise, records are at *Cumbria Record Office, Carlisle.*
Records less than 100 years old containing personal details are closed to the public.

Alston with Garrigill [6].
B. Min's 1837-1930; ledgers and ac's 1835-1930; letter book 1908-13; w'h. tobacco and snuff reg. 1913-16.
Public Record Office, Kew:
Corres. etc. 1836-71 July, 1883-1904 [MH 12/1557-63]; staff reg. 1837-1921 [MH 9/1].

Bootle [7].
A. Creed reg. (with adm's) 1869-1930.
B. Min's 1837-1930; c'tee min's 1882-1930; ac's 1838-1930.
Public Record Office, Kew:
Corres. etc. 1835-62, Sep. 1871-1900 [MH 12/1565-80]; staff reg. 1837-1921 [MH 9/3].

Brampton [2].
A. Outdoor relief lists 1838-48 (vagrants' 1867-1911); poor rate books 1882-1901; relief order books 1848-94; reg. of outdoor relief (at time of General Strike) 1926; papers re. lunacy cases 1879-1928; reg. of visits to children sent out as appr's or servants 1881-2; reg. of infants received for reward 1909-23; vac. lists 1871-1928; public vac's reg's 1882-98; reg's of successful vac's 1853-72; valuation lists 1863-1909; relieving officer's appl. and report books 1867-1929.
B. Min's 1837-1930; ac's 1837-1930; letter books 1837-1923; stat. returns 1838-1925; relieving officer's: receipt and exp. books 1858-1930, entry books 1877-99, pay book 1914-18; parish overseers' records 1887-1927; schedule of extra relief granted because of cotton famine 1867; relief vouchers 1864-90; vac. officer's report books 1898-1921.
Public Record Office, Kew:
Corres. etc. 1834-55, 1860-1900 [MH 12/1581-91]; staff reg. 1837-1921 [MH 9/3].

Carlisle [3].
A. Reg. of paupers 1906-7; appr. indentures 1885-1907; reg. of children under control or adopted or boarded-out 1912-55; children's reg. and relief list 1927-46.
B. Min's (printed) 1897-1930; corres. 1837-98; papers re. building of new w'h. 1861-64; matrons' reports and journals from two children's homes 1924-48.
Carlisle Library:
A. Min's (printed) 1897-1929 (naming maintenance cases, deaths, discharges; annual indexes).
Public Record Office, Kew:
Corres. etc. 1850-1900 [MH 12/1593-617]; staff reg. 1837-1921 [MH 9/4].

Cockermouth [8].
A. Births and deaths reg's 1842-1933; adm. and discharge reg's 1907-27; creed reg's 1904-33; punishment book 1864-1917; reg. of non-resident poor 1883-1904; reg. of grants to British wives and children of interned aliens 1914-20; schools: reg. of children 1887-1922, adm. and discharge book 1907-32; children's homes adm. and discharge book 1922-33.
B. Min's 1838-1929; c'tee min's 1877-1930; ac's 1839-1930; staff reg. 1897-1932; stat. returns and PLB papers 1838-1929; pauper classification books 1886-96; master's day and report books 1925-33; MO's report and statement book 1923-33; children's homes: master's report books 1926-33, clerk's letter books 1924-30.
Public Record Office, Kew:
Corres. etc. 1834-1900 [MH 12/1624-64]; staff reg. 1837-1921 [MH 9/5].

Longtown [1] (incl. pre-1834 records).
B. Min's 1913-30; ac's 1912-30; vouchers and stat. returns 1849-86; misc. incl. re. appointment of officials and Guardians 1787-1895.
Public Record Office, Kew:
Corres. etc. 1834-1899 [MH 12/1675-83]; staff reg. 1837-1921 [MH 9/10].

Penrith [5].
A. Adm's and discharges 1873-1955 (casual paupers 1909-51); births reg. 1837-1935; deaths reg. 1837-1945; post mortems 1897-1931; punishment books 1884-1947; creed reg's 1900-26; lunatic pauper detention orders 1895-1926; reg. of mechanical restraint 1899-1920; relief lists 1869-1952.
B. Min's 1836-1930; c'tee min's 1862-1930; ac's 1871-1930; master's: day books 1898-1945, summaries 1902-56, report books 1913-48, half-yearly reports 1914-27; Lark Hall day books 1915-30; lunatic pauper detention officer's records 1914-61; papers re. w'h. building 1895-c.1945.
Public Record Office, Kew:
Corres. etc. 1834-1900 [MH 12/1684-701]; staff reg. 1837-1921 [MH 9/13].

Whitehaven [9].
A. Births reg. 1856-1906; deaths reg. 1856-1905; adm. and discharge reg's 1893-1962; reg's of children (children's homes) 1924-31; outdoor relief lists 1839-41; reg. of boarded-out children 1910-29.
B. Min's 1860-1931; c'tee min's 1908-31; ac's 1877-1930; staff reg. 1897-1930; stat. returns 1888-1927; letter books 1878-1930; master's reports and journals 1922-26.
Daniel Hay Library, Whitehaven.
A. Persons receiving relief, township of Whitehaven (also ac's, select vestry and officers) 1836.
B. Annual reports, Whitehaven t'ship 1810-12.
Public Record Office, Kew:
Corres. etc. 1834-1900 [MH 12/1706-40]; staff reg. 1837-1921 [MH 9/18].

Cumberland continued

Wigtown (or Wigton) [4].
A. Vagrants' relief book 1879-1880.
B. Min's 1925-30; ac's 1923-1930.
Public Record Office, Kew:
Corres. etc. 1837-1900 [MH 12/1748-67]; staff reg.
1837-1921 [MH 9/19].

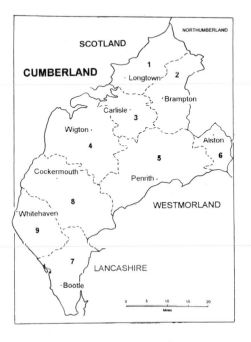

DERBYSHIRE

Unless shown otherwise, records are at
Derbyshire Record Office, Matlock. See
Derbyshire: Guide to the Record Office, 1994,
pp.35-36.

Ashbourne [18] (partly Staffs.).
A. Reg. of boarded-out children c.1908-34.
B. Min's 1845-1930; plans etc. 1846-1946.
Public Record Office, Kew:
Corres. etc. 1835-1900 [MH 12/1772-94]; staff reg.
1837-1921 [MH 9/1].

Ashby-de-la-Zouch [17] (Appleby, The Boundary,
Calke, Hartshorne, Measham, Netherseal (from
1894), Oakthorpe and Donisthorpe, Overseal (from
1894), Packington, Ravenstone (to 1884), Smisby,
Stretton en le Field, Ticknall, Willesley, Woodville
(from 1897)).
See under Leicestershire.

Derbyshire continued

Bakewell [4].
A. Adm. and discharge reg. 1896-7.
B. Min's 1838-1930; C'tee min's: House 1897-
1930, Boarding-out 1912-26; ledgers 1839-1925;
parochial ledgers 1890-1924; terrier of lands c.1839;
documents retained by Derbys. C.C. 1838-1920.
Public Record Office, Kew:
Corres. etc. 1834-1900 [MH 12/1799-828]; staff
reg. 1837-1921 [MH 9/2].

Basford [11] (Codnor and Loscoe, Codnor Park,
Heanor, Ilkeston, Shipley).
See under Nottinghamshire.

Belper [10].
A. Adm. and discharge reg's 1840-50, 1853-1911;
creed reg's 1869-83; births reg's 1840-1957; deaths
reg's 1840-1914.
B. Min's 1837-1930; C'tee min's: House 1900-14,
Children's 1904-29; ledgers 1842-1923; parochial
ledgers 1848-1917; LGB letters 1879-1916;
statement of ac's 1879-1928; MoH annual reports
1873-1916; documents retained by Derbys. C.C.
1837-1910; maps 1880; collector's ledgers 1906-17;
summary of vac. officer's proceedings 1906-12.
Public Record Office, Kew:
Corres. etc. 1833[sic]-1900 [MH 12/1840-80]; staff
reg.1837-1921 [MH 9/2].

Burton-upon-Trent [13] (Ash, Barton Blount,
Bearwardcote, Bretby, Church Broughton,
Burnaston, Caldwell, Catton, Coton in the Elms,
Balbury Lees, Drakelow, Egginton, Etwall, Finsdern,
Foremark, Foston and Scropton, Castle Gresley,
Hatton, Hilton, Ingleby, Linton, Lullington, Marston
on Dove, Mickleover, Newton Solney, Osleton and
Thurvaston, Radbourne, Repton, Rosliston, Stanton
and Newhall, Stapenhill, Sutton on the Hill, Swad-
lincote, Trusley, Twyford and Stenson, Walton upon
Trent, Willington, Winshill).
See under Staffordshire.

Chapel-en-le-Frith [3].
A. Births reg. 1914-48; deaths reg. 1914-43; creed
reg's 1902-25.
B. Min's 1918-30; loose papers 1837-1928; tenders'
1930; Visiting C'tee book 1927-42; w'h. minor ac's
1925-58.
Public Record Office, Kew:
Corres. etc. 1834-1900 [MH 12/1891-914]; staff
reg. 1837-1921 [MH 9/4].

Chesterfield [6].
A. Reg. of visits to appr's (boys) 1881-99; receipts
and exp. 1910-15; appl's and report books
(Chesterfield) 1875-82; adm. and discharge reg's
1838-1946; births reg's 1847-1914; deaths reg's
1838-1904; offences and punishment book 1914-48;
reg. of seclusion and restraint 1914-48.

Derbyshire: Chesterfield *continued*

B. Min's 1837-1930; C'tee min's: House 1908-30, Finance 1906-30, Children's Homes 1912-30, Boarding-out 1910-30, Assessment 1876-1919, SAC 1877-1903; letter books 1911-17; weekly returns 1925-27; ledgers 1839-1929; parochial ledgers 1845-1909; finance books 1912-30; RSA ledgers 1873-77; w'h. building papers 1837-40; title deeds 1776-1838; provisions consumption ac's 1909; collector's ledger (Chesterfield) 1923-26.

Public Record Office, Kew:
Corres. etc. 1834-1900 [MH 12/1920-69]; staff reg. 1837-1921 [MH 9/4].

Derby [14].
A. Manor Hospital creed reg's 1922-31.
B. Manor Hospital religious services reg. 1912-55.
Derby Local Studies Library, Derby.
A. Reg. of children under control of Guardians 1902-45; relieving officer weekly report book 1842-48 (microfilmed).
B. Min's 1837-1931 (printed from 1905); C'tee min's (printed from 1905): Asylums 1900-12, Assessment 1874-88, Boarding-out 1910-16, Building 1876-80, 1889-95, Children's 1900-16, Contracts 1896-1922, Dispensary visiting 1886-1915, Farm 1905-16, Finance 1899-116, Finance settlement and out relief 1894-95, Public assistance 1929-48, Payments and settlements 1902-16, SAC 1900-03, Special purposes 1892-1916, Widows etc. advisory 1913-16, W'h. 1893-1917, Derby Union board c'tees 1916-30, misc. 1920-26; dispensary stock and ac's 1868-70; dispensary visitors' book 1901-46; Derby area housing schemes, contractors' letter book 1920-24; governor's reports 1839-42; letter books 1837-42, 1864-75; press cuttings books: staff advertisements 1894-1906; articles about Derby Board of Guardians 1900-22.

Public Record Office, Kew:
Corres. etc. 1834-1900 [MH 12/1984-2013]; staff reg. 1837-1921 [MH 9/6].

Ecclesall Bierlow [5] (Beauchief, Dore, Norton, Totley).
See under Yorkshire West Riding.

Glossop [1].
B. Draft min's 1842-46.
Public Record Office, Kew:
Corres. etc. 1835-1900 [MH 12/2021-36]; staff reg. 1837-1921 [MH 9/7].

Hayfield [2] (partly Cheshire).
A. Creed reg. 1900-14.
B. Min's 1837-1930 (gaps).
Public Record Office, Kew:
Corres. etc. 1834-1900 [MH 12/2040-57]; staff reg. 1837-1921 [MH 9/8].

Mansfield [9] (Ault Hucknall, Blackwell, Glapwell, Upper Langwith, South Normanton, Pinxton, Pleasley, Scarcliffe, Chirebrook, Tibshelf).
See under Nottinghamshire.

Rotherham [7] (Beighton).
See under Yorkshire West Riding.

Shardlow [15] (partly Leics., Notts.).
A. Ac's of salaries paid to teachers 1894-1920.
B. Min's 1837-90; C'tee min's: Repayment and settlement 1906-30, Assessment 1862-1901, SAC 1877-1909, Shardlow Joint Hospital District 1895-1913; ledgers 1836-38 (unfit for production), 1899-1903; parochial ledger 1908-12; financial statements 1890-94; printed ac's 1895-1915; receipt and exp. book 1922-24; hospital c'tee treasurer's ac's 1910-17; relieving officer, Spondon District, receipt and exp. book 1915-17; master's clothing materials receipt and conversion ac's 1915-50.

Public Record Office, Kew:
Corres. etc. 1834-1900 [MH 12/2060-88]; staff reg. 1837-1921 [MH 9/15].

Tamworth [16] (Chilcote, Croxall).
See under Staffordshire.

Uttoxeter [12] (Boyleston, Cubley, Doveridge, Marston Montgomery, Norbury and Roston, Somersal Herbert, Sudbury).
See under Staffordshire.

Worksop [8] (Barlborough, Clowne, Elmton, Whitwell).
See under Nottinghamshire.

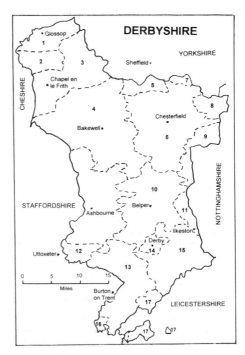

Co. DURHAM

Note. Records at **Durham County Record Office,** *Durham,* containing information on named individuals are closed for 100 years (asterisked), all others for 30 years. Holdings at **Tyne and Wear Archives Service,** *Newcastle upon Tyne,* are abbreviated lists only.

(Bishop) Auckland [11].
Durham County Record Office, *Durham:*
A. Reg. of appr's 1875-97; rate book 1893; poor rate assessments (Bishop Auckland) 1867-8, 1878-9, 1882, (Coundon 1850); valuation lists, various districts, from 1897.
B. Min's 1863-66, 1889-1930; return of salaries 1883-89 (gaps); service reg's 1897-1930; ledger 1898-1904, 1926-29; impersonal ac's 1905-39, personal ac's 1905-43; Joint Hospital Board min's 1895-1948; treasurers' ac's 1911-14; unpaid rates statement 1888-1927; Bishop Auckland overseers' balance ac's 1913-27; Assessment C'tee min's 1881-87, 1895-1901, 1917-23 and letter book 1900-08.
Public Record Office, *Kew:*
Corres. etc. 1834-1900 [MH 12/2928-60]; staff reg. 1837-1921 [MH 9/1].

Belford (Elwick, Ross, to 1844).
See under Northumberland.

Berwick (most places were technically in Co. Durham until 1844).
See under Northumberland.

Chester-le-Street [4].
Durham County Record Office, *Durham:*
This collection is very large, numbering 346 items, and many minor papers have been omitted from this list.
A. Appl's for relief 1929-30; out relief forms for unemployed 1929; reg. and papers re. outdoor relief 1929-30*; relief order books 1928-30 (Chester 1930, Washington 1914-15); Chester bastardy file 1910-30; Boarding-out c'tee: schoolmaster's reports 1911-21, 1925-29*; reg. of cowkeepers, dairymen and milk purveyors 1887-1910; lists of Chester people in receipt of relief 1913-4, 1917-19, 1927-29; County Asylum notices of adm. 1913-28*; lists of lunatics 1923-27* and deaths 1907-13; collectors' receipts and payments 1929-30; valuation lists, various parishes C19-20; papers re. relief to relatives of interned aliens 1914-20*; various lunatics files 1918-28*.
B. Min's 1840-1930 (gaps); agendas 1924-26; C'tee min's: Visiting 1912-15, 1920-26*, Boarding-out 1921-30, Special 1904-13, SAC 1877-90, Assessment 1862-94, (1897-1903 rough), Finance 1913-29; declarations of office 1910-25; four districts relief min's early C20 (closed until 1997); assessment of collieries 1878-87, 1915-20; financial statements 1895-1926; statement of loan ac's 1891-1911; treasurer's ac's 1905-15, receipts and exp.

1926; ledgers 1853-92, 1895-1924; parochial ledgers 1853-1927; non-resident ledger 1888-91; parish estimates 1894-1915; relieving officer's receipts and exp. 1927-29; number and maintenance of pauper lunatics 1912-14; weekly returns of stat's 1914-19; sup'an. reg. 1897-1906; Chester MoH annual reports 1912-14, 1917-8; annual report of sanitary inspectors 1912; byelaws re. new streets and buildings 1911; Chester parish overseers' min's 1923-27; large file of corres. and reports, C20, incl. industrial; cases and appl. for relief 1920-30*; loan ac's sheets and rents 1920s; service reg. 1906-30.
Public Record Office, *Kew:*
Corres. etc. 1836-1900 [MH 12/2968-85]; staff reg. 1837-1921 [MH 9/4].

Darlington [14] (partly Yorkshire N.R.).
Durham County Record Office, *Durham:*
A. Valuation lists 1863-1929; rate books 1840-1910; adm. and discharge reg's 1912-58; creed reg's c.1900-50; births reg. 1911-39; deaths reg's 1877-1974, misc. records re. inmates 1871-95.
B. Min's 1837-1930; C'tee min's: SAC 1877-1904, Visiting 1887-1925, Boarding-out 1889-97, Children 1910-30, Institutions 1925-30, Assessment 1862-1930; rough reports 1919-30; letter books 1852, 1915-28; ledgers 1837, 1904-30; reg. of securities 1869-1930; financial statements 1879-1928, statements of ac's 1889-1915; staff service reg. c.1897-1920; salaries 1905-30; Guardians' declarations of acceptance 1908-28; weekly returns outdoor relief (Northern) 1927-29; newspaper cuttings 1891-1902; list of assistant nurses c.1928; photo of Board 1930; overseers' balance books 1903-27; names and addresses of overseers 1919-27; w'h. ac's and day books 1895-1935; weekly and half-yearly reports 1927-48; wages ac's books 1918-37; stock etc. reg. 1910-43; out letters 1871-95; photos, soldiers and nurses c.1914-19; letters etc. re. examinations and removal orders 1842-1939 (incl. child emigration to Canada 1882-98); half-yearly statements on pauperism 1907-12.
Darlington Branch Library:
Notes on PL in Darlington from 1929 (typescript, 6pp.); 'Resolutions... re. PLUs of Darlington and Teesdale.'
Public Record Office, *Kew:*
Corres. etc. 1834-1900 [MH 12/2989-3014]; staff reg. 1837-1921 [MH 9/6].

Durham [8].
Durham County Record Office, *Durham:*
A. Deaths reg. 1866-1914; reg. of inmates 1925-42; creed reg's c.1925-40; various valuation lists, C18-19.
B. Min's 1837-1902 (gaps); chaplain's report book 1927-65.
Public Record Office, *Kew:*
Corres. etc. 1834-47, 1852-1900 [MH 12/3018-47]; staff reg. 1837-1921 [MH 9/6].

Durham continued

Easington [9].
Durham County Record Office, Durham:
B. Min's 1837-47, 1862-1930; C'tee min's: General 1898-1910, Finance 1903-23, Assessment 1909-14, Relief (North 1898-1930, Mid 1925-31, South 1905-33), Ladies Visiting 1895-1926, Boarding-out 1910-25*, Hospital 1897-1939, House and Buildings 1916-32; ledger 1917-23.
Public Record Office, Kew:
Corres. etc. 1834-1900 [MH 12/3052-65]; staff reg. 1837-1921 [MH 9/6].

Gateshead [1].
Tyne and Wear Archives Service, Newcastle upon Tyne:
A. Reg. of children in homes 1908-49; vac. reg's (Whickham) 1872-1912; infectious diseases reg's (Whickham) 1912-62.
B. Min's 1836-1930.
Gateshead Central Library:
B. Receipts and exp. 1863 (printed).
Newcastle upon Tyne Central Library:
A. Union book (incl. details of paupers) for St. Paul's Church, Winlaton, 1841-55.
Public Record Office, Kew:
Corres. etc. 1834-1900 [MH 12/3068-112]; staff reg. 1837-1921 [MH 9/7].

Hartlepool.
Cleveland County Archives Department, Middlesbrough:
A. Adm. and discharge reg's 1876-1930.
Public Record Office, Kew:
Corres. etc. 1859-1900 [MH 12/3119-40]; staff reg. 1837-1921 [MH 9/8].

Houghton-le-Spring [6].
Durham County Record Office, Durham:
B. Min's 1837-1930; C'tee min's: Finance 1894-1915, Relief 1903-30 (gaps, 75 year closure), Assessment 1862-1907, Boarding-out 1920-30*, House 1918-35; Heath House inmates' property 1908-60*.
Public Record Office, Kew:
Corres. etc. 1834-1900 [MH 12/3147-61]; staff reg. 1837-1921 [MH 9/9].

Lanchester [3].
Durham County Record Office, Durham:
B. Service reg. 1902-30.
Public Record Office, Kew:
Corres. etc. 1835-74, 1881-86 May, 1888-1900 [MH 12/3165-81]; staff reg. 1837-1921 [MH 9/10].

Monkwearmouth (pre-1834).
Tyne and Wear Archives Service, Newcastle upon Tyne:
A. Adm. and discharge reg's 1813-36; settlement, bastardy and removal papers 1807-43.

Sedgefield [12].
Durham County Record Office, Durham:
A. Births reg. 1837-48, 1857-1929; deaths reg. 1838-48, 1866-1930; creed reg's 1869-1927 (some closed); Boarding-out reg's 1911-27*; MO's exam's 1910-43*; lunatic cert's 1881-1909*; adm. and discharge reg's 1837-98 (1916-36 closed); adm. and discharge reg's, casual paupers, 1871-73, 1878-1914 (+1914-35 closed); indoor relief lists 1836-67, 1874-1914 (+1914-58 closed); appl. and report books 1927-32*; outdoor relief list, abstract 1916-30, lists 1921-43 (both closed); relief order books 1923-4, 1926*; creed reg's 1869-89, 1904-14; reg. of lunatics in asylum and annual returns of lunatics 1906-30*; reg. of young persons placed in service 1875-88; payments for children boarded-out 1912-30*; reg. of persons receiving infants for reward 1923-38*; collector's receipt and payment 1922-30.
B. Boarding-out C'tee min's 1912-23*; ledger 1843-47; parochial ledger 1908-27; financial statements 1915-30; Forms A and B 1925-29/30; letter books 1926-30; master's reports and journals 1847-56, 1864-1941 (gaps); half-yearly reports 1914-45; Visiting C'tee reports 1893-1905, 1920-29; Lunatic Visiting C'tee min's 1912-33*; treasurer's receipts and exp. 1925-30; collector's ledgers 1924-30; relieving officers' receipts and exp. 1923-27, 1929-30; master's report and journal 1872-74; master's receipts and exp. 1917-30; reg. of mortgages etc. 1926-7; porters' books 1910-13.
Public Record Office, Kew:
Corres. etc. 1834-66, 1871 Sep-1900 [MH 12/3188-99]; staff reg. 1837-1921 [MH 9/15].

South Shields [2].
Tyne and Wear Archives Service, Newcastle upon Tyne:
A. Epileptic reg's 1911-36; lunacy reg's 1908-48; birth reg's 1914-37; death reg's 1914-48; adm's 1926-48; creed reg's 1877-1948; adm. and discharge books 1897-1956.
B. Min's (printed) 1899-1932 (also at *South Shields Central Library*).
Public Record Office, Kew:
Corres. etc. 1834-1900 [MH 12/3201-32]; staff reg. 1837-1921 [MH 9/15].

Stockton [13] (partly Yorkshire N.R.).
Durham County Record Office, Durham:
A. Adm. and discharge reg's 1915-32; reg's of children 1900-46; reg. of children in employment 1911-29; outdoor relief lists 1887-1912 (+1923-4 closed); East District school fees appl. and report book 1884-5.
B. Min's 1888-91, 1895-1930; Assessment C'tee min's 1862-1928 (some in rough); appl. and report books (East) 1882-1903; w'h. plans c.1851; many plans and property details, C19; Children's homes: superintendants' report etc. 1911-29; service reg's 1897-1930; salaries books 1908-11.
Public Record Office, Kew:
Corres. etc. 1843-59, 1864-1900 [MH 12/3241-64]; staff reg. 1837-1921 [MH 9/16].

Sunderland [5].
Tyne and Wear Archives Service, Newcastle upon Tyne:
A. Creed reg's 1888-1941; indoor relief lists 1866-1947; reg's of male and female lunatics 1896-1948; death reg's 1866-1954.
Public Record Office, Kew:
Corres. etc. 1834-62, 1867-1900 [MH 12/3268-304]; staff reg. 1837-1921 [MH 9/16].

Teesdale [10] (partly Yorkshire N.R.).
Durham County Record Office, Durham:
A. Rating and assessment books 1851-84 (gaps); collecting and deposit books 1879-88.
B. Dietary tables 1901.
Public Record Office, Kew:
Corres. etc. 1834-42, 1851-1900 [MH 12/3313-44]; staff reg. 1837-1921 [MH 9/17].

Tynemouth see Northumberland.

Weardale [7].
Durham County Record Office, Durham:
A. Poor rate books (+ statements, collecting books, highway rates, some lists of indoor and outdoor poor etc.): Wolsingham 1834-1917 (gaps), Tow Law 1895-1918; Wolsingham special expense rate 1878-1918 and valuation lists 1865-97 (gaps).
B. Min's 1865; half-yearly ac's 1837-1903; monthly statements 1869-75, 1883-1912.
Public Record Office, Kew:
Corres. etc. 1834-82, 1886-1900 [MH 12/3333-44]; staff reg. 1837-1921 [MH 9/18].

Northern Counties Poor Law Committee.
Durham County Record Office, Durham:
B. Min's 1912-30.
Public Record Office, Kew:
Staff reg. 1914-19 [MH 9/20].

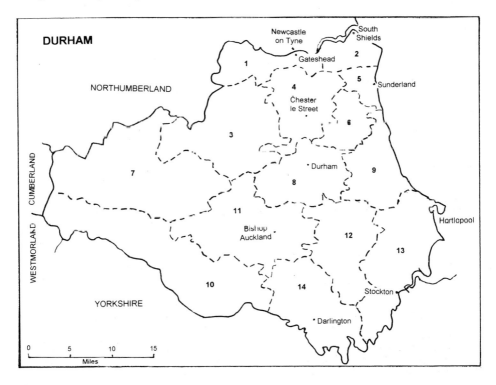

LANCASHIRE

See A.A. Todd, '1843 return of sponsored poor law migrants', *Lancashire* **6**, 2, May 1985; R. Hirst, 'Pauper migration', *Lancashire* **6**, 3, Autumn 1985; T. Benton, '"Here is a living and a good one": Movement to Lancashire and Cheshire under the 1835-37 sponsored Poor Law Migration Scheme', *Lancashire*, **7**, 1, Feb. 1986.

Ashton under Lyne [23] (partly in Cheshire).
Lancashire Record Office, Preston:
B. Constitution 1837; Min's 1837-1930 (the remainder of this PLU's records were pulped during World War 2).
Public Record Office, Kew:
Corres. etc. 1834-1900 (missing 1855-6, July - Dec. 1859, 1863, Aug. 1871-72, Jan.- May 1886) [MH 12/5413-57]; staff reg. 1837-1921 [MH 9/1].

Barrow-in-Furness [1] (a separate union from 1872; see also **Ulverston**).
Cumbria Record Office, Barrow-in-Furness (* denotes restricted access):
A. Reg. of persons in receipt of relief 1929-30*; reg. of persons in institutions, 1927-29 (weekly returns); w'h. adm's register 1876-1949 (mostly *); creed reg's 1871-81, 1913-30*; death reg's 1876-1942*;
B. Min's 1876-80; overseers' min's 1876-1927; unlisted c'tee papers, cash books etc., mostly C20; w'h. inventory books 1923-50; w'h. plans 1888-1914; reports on vagrancy in Barrow 1870.
Public Record Office, Kew:
Corres. etc. 1836-1900 (missing 1836- Feb. 1886) [MH 12/5475-85]; staff reg. 1837-1921 [MH 9/3].

Barton-upon-Irwell [26].
Lancashire Record Office, Preston:
A. Outdoor relief lists 1850-70; births reg. 1868-1928; deaths reg. 1909-14; creed reg. 1913-19, 1922-29.
B. Constitution 1849; min's 1849-1930; Assessment C'tee min's 1862-1927; MO's report book 1926-43; RSA min's 1872-94 and ledgers 1873-94.
Public Record Office, Kew:
Corres. etc. 1840-1900 (missing 1856-58, 1869-Aug. 1871, 1883, 1891-2) [MH 12/5486-514]; staff reg. 1837-1921 [MH 9/2].

Blackburn [6].
Lancashire Record Office, Preston:
A. Queen's Park reg's (1885-1913 chronological, 1894-1949 alphabetical); death reg's 1914-30; inmates' property reg's 1914-33; children's reg's 1921-43; reg's of mechanical restraint 1906-59; reg's of seclusion 1914-59; operations record 1920-39; reg. of lunacy patients 1920-59.
B. Min's 1837-1930; C'tee min's: Finance 1863-97, Finance and Salaries 1897-1928, Stores 1899-1930, SAC 1877-1903, Cottage Homes 1900-30, W'h. Farming 1890-1922, Boarding-out 1910-30, RSA 1873-94, misc. 1897-1925; ledgers 1837-1930,

parochial ledgers 1864-1927; Queen's Park: reports 1927-45, index of officers 1882-1942; wages receipt books 1916-22.
Blackburn District Central Library:
B. Rent book 1886-1923; c'tee report on children in w'h. 1893; salaries books 1895-1906; ac's 1920-48; Guardian attendance book ? -1930; Finance C'tee min's 1928-30; other c'tee min's 1926-30; staff reg. 1896-1920.
Public Record Office, Kew:
Corres. etc. 1834-1900 (missing 1874, July - Dec. 1881, Jan.- June 1892) [MH 12/5529-75]; staff reg. 1837-1921 [MH 9/2].

Blackrod see **Horwich.**

Bolton [11].
Bolton Archive Service, Bolton:
A. Indoor and outdoor relief reg's 1839-1930; valuation lists 1911-21; w'h. adm's and discharges 1839-1930; births and deaths reg's 1839-1941; creed reg's 1869-1930.
B. Min's 1837-1930; C'tee min's 1843-1930; corres. etc. 1865-1930; newspaper cuttings 1864-1930; nurses' reg's 1889-1928; officers' appointment books 1870-1888; personnel files 1870-1930; financial records 1839-1930.
Public Record Office, Kew:
Corres. etc. 1834-1900 (missing 1847, 1849, 1852-54, Jan.- June 1859, Jan.- May 1890) [MH 12/5593-655]; staff reg. 1837-1921 [MH 9/3].

Burnley [7].
Lancashire Record Office, Preston:
A. Valuation lists 1875-1929; reg's of children 1904-10, 1928-45.
B. Constitution 1836; min's 1837-1930; C'tee min's: Assessment 1862-1920, W'h. building 1871-77, SAC 1877-97, General 1879-1905, RSA 1872-82, 1891-4.
Burnley District Central Library:
A. Adm. and discharge reg. 1911; creed reg's and index to adm. and discharge books 1906-30; reg's. of inmates' relatives: males 1876-1901 (mostly 1900-1), females 1879-1908 (mostly 1907-8); monthly reports on children boarded-out 1921-30; outdoor relief lists: Dist. 1 1910-21, Dist. 2 1887-1930, Dist. 3 1910-28, Dist. 4 1929-30; working boys' home: reg. of inmates 1925-40, adm. and discharge reg. 1925-42; Primrose Bank Institution creed reg's 1894-1943.
B. Constitution 1836; min's 1843-48, 1907; year book 1882-3; corres. 1895-1920; papers re. elections of Guardians 1869, 1904; weekly returns (form A) 1929-31; plan of w'h. extension 1904; instructions re. valuation 1884.
Public Record Office, Kew:
Corres. etc. 1834-1900 (missing 1847, 1854-56, 1863-66, 1879, Sep.- Feb. 1881, Oct. 1881- Aug. 1883, June 1884- June 1885, Jan.- June 1889, Jan.- May 1890, Jan.- July 1891) [MH 12/5673-710]; staff reg. 1837-1921 [MH 9/3].

Burscough see **Ormskirk.**

Lancashire continued

Bury [13].

Lancashire Record Office, Preston (records may be sent to Bury Public Library Archives Dept. in the near future):

B. Min's 1840-1930; returns of paupers relieved 1871-1900; returns of Guardians and officials 1870-1915; voucher book 1848-58; bills 1848-51.

Public Record Office, Kew:
Corres. etc. 1847- Sep. 1883 (missing 1855-60, 1863-76, 1878- Feb. 1883) [MH 12/5730-36]; staff reg. 1837-1921 [MH 9/3].

Caton [25] (Gilbert Union until 1869; then see Lunesdale).

Lancashire Record Office, Preston:
A. Poor rate assessments 1851-83.
B. W'h. ac's 1830-40; misc. w'h. papers c.1869-75.

Chorley [9].

Lancashire Record Office, Preston:
A. Punishment records 1872-1948; valuations: Adlington 1863-1920, Chorley 1873-78, Leyland 1863-1907; lists of paupers 1899-1900; adm. and discharge records 1926-52; reg. of mechanical restraint 1901-48.

B. Min's 1861-2, 1878-82, 1901-30; C'tee min's: Assessment 1862-70, 1897-1927, RSA 1880-94, others 1912-30, master's reports 1913-47, letter books 1077-95, 1910-30, ledgers 1843-1927, parochial ledgers 1854-1897; rechargeable paupers' ledger 1842-45; rating papers 1894-1927.

Public Record Office, Kew:
Corres. etc. 1834-1896 (missing 1834-48, 1851-85, July 1887-92) [MH 12/5738-42]; staff reg. 1837-1921 [MH 9/5].

Chorlton (South Manchester) [21].

Manchester City Archives:
A. List of emigrant children to Canada and other countries 1889-1947 (indexed).
B. Abstract of ac's (printed) 1838-1915; weekly returns 1843-1915 (gaps); LGB letters 1905, 1910; ledgers 1837-1915 (gaps); loan ledger 1910-30.

Public Record Office, Kew:
Corres. etc. 1834-1897 (missing 1834-62, June 1863-68, 1870- Jan. 1889, Aug. 1889- Mar. 1892, 1893-4, 1896 [MH 12/5743-48]; staff reg. 1837-1921 [MH 9/5 and 20].

Chorlton & Manchester Joint Asylum Committee.

Manchester City Archives:
B. Ledgers 1897-1913.

Chorlton and Manchester Joint W'h. Committee.

Manchester City Archives:
B. Ledgers 1902-12.

Clitheroe [4] (partly Yorks. West Riding).

Lancashire Record Office, Preston:
A. Births reg. 1867-1915; deaths reg. 1866-1914; relief order book 1924-1930; creed reg. 1914-34; reg. of mechanical restraint 1901-48.

B. Min's 1837-1902, 1905-30; C'tee min's: Buildings 1870-74, SAC 1877-86, RSA 1880-94; letter books 1843-1940; ledgers 1838-47, 1874-1908; township ac's books 1838-1909; MO's report books 1926-55; cash reg. 1897-1961.

Public Record Office, Kew:
Corres. etc. 1834-1900 (missing 1857-59, 1889-96) [MH 12/5752-64]; staff reg. 1837-1921 [MH 9/5].

Derby, West see West Derby.

Fylde [3].

Lancashire Record Office, Preston:
B. Min's 1845-1930; C'tee min's: Assessment 1862-1927, W'h. 1864-1930, Finance 1906-30, Children's Homes 1908-19, Boarding-out 1911-46, Cottage Homes 1920-30, RSA 1873-94.

Public Record Office, Kew:
Corres. etc. 1834-1900 (missing 1834-62, 1879, 1883) [MH 12/5766-99]; staff reg. 1837-1921 [MH 9/7].

Fylde, Preston and Garstang Joint Board.

Lancashire Record Office, Preston:
B. Min's 1896-1918

Garstang [2].

Lancashire Record Office, Preston:
B. Min's 1837-1930; C'tee min's: Assessment 1862-64, SAC 1877-1903, W'h. Management 1908-14, House 1914-30, RSA 1873-91; ledgers 1902-30.

Public Record Office, Kew:
Corres. etc. 1844-1900 (missing 1851-55) [MH 12/5825-39]; staff reg. 1837-1921 [MH 9/7].
See also under **Fylde**.

Haslingden [12].

Lancashire Record Office, Preston:
A. Valuations 1880-82.
B. Min's 1838-1930; C'tee min's: W'h. 1865-70, RSA 1872-83 (with letter book 1873-80), Infirmary 1898-1905, Boarding-out 1911-20; letter books 1838-1902; lists of Guardians and officers 1839-1921; year books 1904-29; overseers' balance sheets 1856-88, 1917-25.

Rawtenstall District Central Library:
Higher Booths Township: rate assessments 1846, 1871, 1880, parochial c'tee min's 1875-83; Rawtenstall relief fund papers 1862-3; Rawtenstall No. 2 Dist. rate book 1912.

Public Record Office, Kew:
Corres. etc. 1834-1900 (missing 1851-55, 1859, 1890) [MH 12/5840-78]; staff reg. 1837-1921 [MH 9/8].

Horwich, Westhoughton & Blackrod Joint Board.

Lancashire Record Office, Preston:
B. Min's 1909-39; ledgers 1901-09, 1915-28.

Kendal (Dalton).

See under Westmorland.

Lancashire continued

Lancaster [25] (from 1869 incl. **Caton**).
Lancashire Record Office, Preston:
A. Relief books 1894-1945; vac. records 1857-66, 1885-1915; pauper lunatic records 1865-1923; Parkside Inst. births reg. 1914-58; creed reg. 1926-46; diseases reg. 1920-51.
B. Constitution 1839; min's 1839-1930; C'tee min's: W'h. 1840-45, 1918-28, Children's Home 1910-28, RSA 1872-94, Finance 1889-1928, Assessment 1866-69 (with letter books), General 1928-30; letter books: registration 1841-44, general 1845-69, 1887-1920; lists of Guardians and officers 1840-1904; ledgers 1918-30; abstracts of ac's 1892-1903, 1912-1913; overseers' balance sheets 1903-25.
Public Record Office, Kew:
Corres. etc. 1834-1900 (missing 1854-56) [MH 12/5889-914]; staff reg. 1837-1921 [MH 9/10 (Lancaster), MH 9/4 (Caton)].

Lathom see **Ormskirk**.

Leigh [19].
Wigan Record Office, Leigh:
A. Asylum reception orders, various, 1879-1940 (closed 75 years); removal orders 1898-1928 (closed 75 years); rate books, various townships between 1863 and 1894; reg. of Rural SAC C'tee labour cert's 1883-1905.
B. PLC orders 1837; Min's 1837-1930; Assessment C'tee min's 1886-1904 and letter book 1923-38; township plans 1864-81; SAC officer's reports 1893-1912, report book 1914-25 and misc. papers 1920-25; deeds 1822, 1850; PLB circulars re. sale of Lowton w'h. 1850-55.
Lancashire Record Office, Preston:
B. RSA min's 1873-90.
Public Record Office, Kew:
Corres. etc. 1834-1900 (missing 1844-49, Aug. 1891- Apr. 1892) [MH 12/5926-54]; staff reg. 1837-1921 [MH 9/10].

Liverpool [28] (Select vestry).
See I. Taylor, 'Liverpool Workhouse records collection', *Liverpool FHS,* **2**, 1, Spring 1978.
Liverpool Record Office:
A. Appr. indentures 1840-70 (indexed); baptisms reg. 1831-58, 1874-1928; adm. reg's 1869-1925; adm. and discharge (or creed) reg's 1841-1928; births reg's 1841-1914; deaths reg's 1914-24; Kirkdale industrial schools: adm. and discharge reg's 1862-1965, classification reg's 1845-97, creed reg's 1869-1904.
B. Min's 1852-1922 (printed from 1911); C'tee min's: Contract and Supply 1861-1911, Finance and General Purposes 1846-1911, Grove Mount 1895-98, Highfield 1906-7, Industrial Schools 1845-1908, Maghull 1878-94, Medical Relief 1850-53, Special Cholera 1866, W'h. 1842-1911; a'c books 1870-1; deeds 1842-68; PLC, PLB, LGB orders 1842-1906.

Public Record Office, Kew:
Corres. etc. 1834-1900 (missing 1841-44, 1847-50, 1853-55, 1857, 1875) [MH 12/5966-6017]; staff reg. 1837-1921 [MH 9/10 and 20].

Lunesdale [25] (formed 1869; see also **Caton**).
Lancashire Record Office, Preston:
B. Min's 1869-1900; C'tee min's: Assessment 1868-96, RSA 1873-92, SAC 1877-97; letter book 1869-71.
Public Record Office, Kew:
Corres. etc. 1869-1900 (missing Aug. 1871-73, 1877-89) [MH 12/6033-37]; staff reg. 1869-1921 [MH 9/10].

Manchester [27] (PLU 1841-50; Parish 1850 on).
See H.M. Boot, 'Unemployment and poor law relief in Manchester 1845-50', *Social History* **15** (1990).
Manchester Central Library, Local Studies Unit:
A. Adm. and discharge reg's 1841-45; creed reg's 1881-1914 (gaps); list of children sent to Swinton industrial school 1846-64; children under control of Guardians (printed) 1929.
B. Weekly returns 1842-1930; ledgers 1894-1930; half-yearly receipts and exp. 1927; ac's (printed) 1849; stat's 1846-51; abstract of ac's (printed) 1851-1914; annual reports (printed) 1915-20.
Lancashire Record Office, Preston:
A. Swinton industrial schools: institution adm. and discharge books 1846-48, 1850-1934, school adm. and discharge books 1892-1926, indexes 1848-1935.
B. Master's journal 1922-29.
Public Record Office, Kew:
Corres. etc. 1837- June 1899 (missing 1848- July 1850, 1851-56, Jan.-June 1858, 1868, Aug. 1871-72, Jan.- Nov. 1889, 1893-4) [MH 12/6039-89]; staff reg. 1837-1921 [MH 9/11 and 20].

Manchester, South see **Chorlton**.

Manchester, Chorlton and, Joint Asylum and W'h. C'tees see **Chorlton**.

Oldham [15].
Oldham Archives Service, Local Studies Library, Oldham.
Some records are in a poor state, and some are subject to a 100-year closure rule).
A. Scattered homes: adm. and discharge reg's 1899-1948, reg. of girls 1896-1934, boys 1900-34; reg. of children received and detained in w'h. 1910-41; hospital adm. and discharge reg's 1871-74, 1878-1951, mental wards (female) 1915-45; alphabetical reg. of mental wards (female) 1890-1904, 1913-19; births reg. 1847-1931; deaths reg. 1887-94, 1917-47; creed reg's 1891-1946 (gaps); reg. of relatives 1888-1945 (gaps); lunatic books 1926-31; reg. of paupers' articles 1913-18; detention orders and lunacy cert's 1909-40; lists of paupers in receipt of relief 1876-1909; various lists of children 1877, 1894-98, 1903, 1905, 1908; various lists of paupers 1880's-1900's; returns of lunatics 1872, 1897-8, 1910-1; lists of patients in Whittingham

County Hospital 1898-1919 (gaps), Lancaster County and Royal Albert Asylums 1896-1919 (gaps), Prestwich 1900-11 (gaps), Winwick 1902-12 (gaps); printed lists of paupers: Crompton 1840-1, Failsworth 1835, Royton 1856; 5 bastardy orders (1890-1904); valuation lists (10 wards) 1912.

B. Min's 1901-30; C'tee min's: Finance 1896-99, 1903-06, Finance and General Purposes 1926-30, Building 1892-1907, 1925-30, W'h. Hospital 1894-1907, House 1927-30, Farm 1893-1906, Visiting 1878-1902, Boarding-out 1919-23, Settlement and Revision 1927-30, Schools 1891-1902, Scattered Homes 1903-09, Children's 1909-13, 1928-30, Cottage Homes 1893-4; reg. of securities 1884-1927; receipts and exp. 1872-75, 1880-99; overseers' reg. 1847; various officers' bonds and contracts 1870's-90's; rate returns 1870-99 (gaps); salaries: MO's 1871-79, teachers' 1871-79, 1890-92; leases, agreements, mortgages between 1849 and 1913; matron's report book 1929-38; porter's books 1907-09, wages books 1888-92, 1900-10, 1914-31; voluminous other papers incl. appeals, High Court action (1899), rating reports etc. C19-20; expenses for: Guardians' visits 1888-1910, w'h. children's visits to seaside 1894-1903; various printed reports 1832-41, ac's and statements incl. reports, contracts, insurances, tenders etc. C19-1905; stat. returns 1872-79, 1892, 1906-7; LGB return of removal expenses 1882-86; returns as to religious ministrations 1879, 1881, and vac's 1878-88, 1896-1903; various provisions ac's between 1832 and 1892; Assessment C'tee yearbook 1928-9.

Lancashire Record Office, Preston:
A. Valuations 1914, 1929.
B. Min's 1837-1901; Assessment C'tee min's 1896-1912.
Public Record Office, Kew:
Corres. etc. 1837-1900 all missing [MH 12]; staff reg. 1837-1921 [MH 9/12].

Ormskirk [8].
Lancashire Record Office, Preston:
B. Min's 1837-1930; C'tee min's: Assessment 1896-1912, RSA 1872-94; Union year book 1914-5.
Public Record Office, Kew:
Corres. etc. 1837-1900 all missing [MH 12]; staff reg. 1837-1921 [MH 9/12].

Ormskirk, Lathom and Burscough Joint Board.
Lancashire Record Office, Preston:
B. Min's 1901-31; ledgers 1902-25.

Prescot [17].
Lancashire Record Office, Preston (microfilm copies at **Huyton Library**):
B. Min's 1837-1930; C'tee min's: RSA 1873-94, Assessment 1862-81, Finance 1894-1911, General 1872-1930, SAC 1877-1903.
Public Record Office, Kew:
Corres. etc. 1834-1900 (missing 1843-46, 1850-83, June 1884- July 1890, Aug. 1891-96) [MH 12/6094-101]; staff reg. 1837-1921 [MH 9/13].

Preston [5].
See 'The sponsored poor law migration scheme 1835-1837 [in Preston]', *Lancashire Local Historian* **6**, 1991.
Lancashire Record Office, Preston:
A. W'h. and Civic Hostel births reg. 1868-93; baptisms reg. 1907-49; Sharoe Green adm. reg. 1926-48.
B. Min's 1838-1930; Assessment C'tee mins 1907-27; overseers' mins 1866-1927; officers' appointment book 1898-1932.
Public Record Office, Kew:
Corres. etc. 1834-1900 (missing 1834-41, 1843-46, 1853-56, 1858, 1861-63, 1866- Aug. 1871, 1880, 1883- May 1884, 1887, 1889- Apr. 1891) [MH 12/6112-37]; staff reg. 1837-1921 [MH 9/13].
See also under **Fylde**.

Prestwich [27] (1850-1930).
Manchester Central Library, Local Studies Unit:
B. Abstract of ac's (printed) 1868-1915 (gaps), year books (printed) 1889-1914 (gaps); weekly returns 1851-1915; ledgers 1862-1913; LGB regulations for infirmary 1909; list of Guardians and officers 1889-1914 (except 1894).
Public Record Office, Kew:
Corres. etc. 1834-1900 (missing 1834-49, Aug. 1871-72, 1877, 1882, Oct. 1887- Dec. 1888) [MH 12/6147-73]; staff reg. 1837-1921 [MH 9/13].

Rochdale [14].
See J. Cole, *Down poorhouse lane. the diary of a Rochdale workhouse* (1984).
Rochdale Central Library (Local Studies):
A. Statement of ac's 1830-1, 1852-87, 1889-1908 (lists those receiving relief); Heywood poor rate 1910-12, 1915-29, valuation lists 1922.
B. Min's 1837-45, 1899-1930; yearbooks 1895-1928.
Lancashire Record Office, Preston:
B. Min's 1845-1900; C'tee min's: Building 1868-77, General Purposes 1874-78, Parliamentary 1887-93, various others 1863-65, 1892-1900, Visiting 1874-94, W'h. 1851-87.
Public Record Office, Kew:
Corres. etc. 1834-1900 (missing 1834-45, 1850-52, 1864, 1873, 1883, 1887) [MH 12/6176-212]; staff reg. 1837-1921 [MH 9/14].

Salford [20].
For the early history of the Union see D.A. Farnie, 'The establishment of the new poor law in Salford, 1838-1850', unpublished thesis (copy at **Salford Local History Library**).
Salford Archives Centre, Irlam:
'Adm. and discharge reg's went for salvage during the second World War.'
B. Min's (indexed) 1838-1930 (missing 1911); C'tee min's (some indexed): W'h. Visiting 1865-1930, Infirmary Visiting 1882-1930, Children's 1899-1930, Boarding-out 1911-16, Relief (various) 1913-30, Old People's Homes Management 1928-30, Finance 1913-29, General Purposes (and sub-c'tees) 1912-

Lancashire: Salford *continued*

22, Stores etc. 1914-29, Works etc. 1922-30, Hospital 1880-1, Hospital Extensions 1929-30, W'h. Building 1897-1903, SAC 1877-95; misc. corres., contracts, spec's 1897-1930; plans 1851-1929.
Public Record Office, Kew:
Corres. etc. 1834-1900 (missing 1834-40, 1877-8) [MH 12/6220-61]; staff reg. 1837-1921 [MH 9/15].

Stockport [22] (Heaton Norris, Reddish).
See under Cheshire.

Todmorden [24] (partly Yorks. W.R.)
Calderdale District Archives, Halifax:
A. Adm. and discharge book 1880-82.
B. Min's 1882-1911; letter book 1837-41; w'h. ac's. 1875-79.
Public Record Office, Kew:
Corres. etc. 1834-1900 (missing 1845-51, 1856-7, 1876) [MH 12/6272-98]; staff reg. 1837-1921 [MH 9/17].

Toxteth Park [28] (1857-1922).
Liverpool Record Office.
B. Min's 1894-1922; Visiting and General Purpose C'tee min's 1891-95, 1910-12, 1921-22; orders of PLC, PL and LG Boards 1837-1915; misc. papers 1867-68, 1919-20.
Public Record Office, Kew:
Corres. etc. 1857-1900 (missing 1857-59, 1861, 1881-2) [MH 12/6299-318]; staff reg. 1837-1921 [MH 9/17].

Ulverston [1] (see also Barrow-in-Furness).
Cumbria Record Office, Barrow (* denotes restricted access):
A. Births reg. 1866-1948*; deaths reg. 1866-1916; reg. of punishments 1874-1923, 1928-45*; reg. of adm's and discharges 1901-03; reg. of relations, n.d. (early C20); reg. of visits by relieving officer to young persons under 16, hired or taken as servants from the w'h. 1863-79.
B. Master's report books 1891-93, 1926-48*; various papers relating to the establishing and running of the w'h., C19/20; PLC orders 1838; w'h. plans 1859-97.
The Barrow Record Office also has overseers' ac's books from Cartmel Fell (1831-36), and Egton cum Newland (1836), incl. exam. of paupers 1866-70, and a SAC census register of Aldingham parish 1888.
Lancashire Record Office, Preston:
A. Reg's of rating objections 1891-1929.
B. Min's 1836-1930; C'tee min's: Assessment 1862-1927, General 1890-1918, House 1920-24, House and Children 1927-30; ledgers 1836-76; parochial ledger 1911-27; letter books 1869-1930; RSA min's 1872-94; General Purposes C'tee min's 1890-1900, nuisance reports 1892-94, ledgers 1872-94, LGB letters 1872-80, 1882-89.
Public Record Office, Kew:
Corres. etc. 1834-1896 (missing 1839-42, 1884-90) [MH 12/6320-44]; staff reg. 1837-1921 [MH 9/17].

Warrington [18].
Lancashire Record Office, Preston:
B. Min's 1837-1900; RSA min's 1872-77, 1883-94; RSA ledgers 1873-95; surveyor's reports 1880-94.
Public Record Office, Kew:
Corres. etc. 1837-1900 (missing 1837-44, 1850-61, 1864-66, Aug. 1871-74, 1877-8, 1882, Sep. 1883-June 1885, Aug. 1886-91, 1893-96) [MH 12/6350-62]; staff reg. 1837-1921 [MH 9/18].

West Derby [16].
Liverpool Record Office:
A. Records of Walton w'h. c.1866-1935.
B. Min's 1848-1930 (indexed 1922-30); C'tee min's: Finance 1883-1923, General Purposes 1871-1922, Visiting 1877-1913, Joint Hospitals 1899-1922, Misc. 1866-1922; ac's books 1852-55, 1900-11; weekly returns of persons relieved 1920-22; misc. 1884-1929; Guardians' declarations of office 1894-1921.
Liverpool Central Library:
B. Min's 1922-30; Assessment C'tee rules 1892; year books 1923/4, 1928/9.
Lancashire Record Office, Preston:
B. RSA min's 1885-94.
Public Record Office, Kew:
Corres. etc. 1837-1899 July (missing 1837-62, 1865- Aug. 1871, Apr. 1872- July 1881, 1882- May 1884, Sep. 1884- Sep. 1888, Apr. 1889- Jan. 1890, 1891- Sep. 1897, June - Dec. 1898) [MH 12/6367-77]; staff reg. 1837-1921 [MH 9/18].

Westhoughton see **Horwich**.

Wigan [10].
Wigan Record Office, Leigh:
A. Relief order books 1891-97; claims for exp. for maintenance of lunatics 1886-7, 1890-1; index to labour cert's for children 1883-88; poll books for election of Guardians 1890-92; Standish appl. and report books 1875-1902 (gaps) and outdoor relief lists 1874-1902 (gaps); Wigan outdoor relief list 1894; Hindley collector's receipt and exp. book 1892-98; Abram receipt and exp. book 1848-67; vac. reg 1899-1909; school fees appl. and report books (Wigan) 1891; reg. of inmates in w'h. 1906-49 (closed 75 years, but staff may undertake searches).
B. Min's 1837-1930; C'tee min's: Finance 1886-89, Assessment 1863-75, Removal 1888-95, RSA (Wigan) 1873-90, SAC 1877-1903 (Estimates 1889-99), W'h. 1884-96, W'h. Building 1856-58, Estate 1882-97; various other committee papers 1877-1930; ledgers 1838-84; treasurer's receipt and exp. books 1882-85, 1889-1901; parochial ledgers 1848-81 (and related books 1873-93); officers' bonds 1838-56; statements of officers' securities 1867-8; clerk's ac's 1867-96; exp.: statement 1867, abstracts 1877-96; annual poor rate returns 1886-7, 1890, 1897; stat. returns 1890-1, 1893-99; misc. returns 1867-71; pauper classification books 1893-1900; deeds re. Hindley w'h. 1830-50; deeds etc. re. Wigan w'h. 1837-58; corres. (incl. PLC etc.) 1833-76; relieving officer (Hindley) receipt and exp. books 1873-78; Standish receipt and exp. books 1886-

28

1902 (gaps); RSA Finance C'tee and Aspull
Parochial C'tee 1873-76; ledger 1873-94; treasurer's
ac's 1880-1902;; special expenses (Aspull 1876,
Haigh 1880-85).

Lancashire Record Office, Preston:
B. Min's 1837-1930; C'tee min's: Assessment
1863-75, Removal 1888-95, SAC 1877-1903, W'h.

1884-96, RSA 1872-94 (with ledgers 1873-94),
various 1896-1930; ledgers 1838-61; abstract of
exp. 1877-96.

Public Record Office, Kew:
 Corres. etc. 1837-1900 (missing 1837-57, 1860-74,
1876-98) [MH 12/6378-81]; staff reg. 1837-1921 [MH
9/19].

LEICESTERSHIRE

Except when shown otherwise, records are at **Leicestershire Record Office,** *Wigston Magna.* There is a 100 year closure on personal records.

Ashby-de-la-Zouch (pre-1834).
B. Min's, house of industry, 1814-26.

Ashby-de-la-Zouch [2] (partly Derbys.).
A. Adm. and discharge reg's 1837-1936 (vagrants 1915-30); births and deaths reg's 1868-1936; medical exam. records 1914-36; creed reg's 1900-36; clothing reg. 1899-1906; addresses of paupers' friends 1904-25; porter's books 1915-29.
B. Min's 1838-1930; ledger 1925-30; letter book 1840-43; service reg's 1878-1928.
Public Record Office, Kew:
Corres. etc. 1834-1900 (missing 1839- Aug. 1871, 1873-76, May 1878 -1881, Aug. 1887-88 [MH 12/6387-96]; staff reg. 1837-1921 [MH 9/1].

Atherstone [8] (Atterton, Fenny Drayton, Merevale, Ratcliffe Culey, Sheepy Magna and Parva, Witherley).
See under Warwickshire.

Barrow-upon-Soar [7].
A. Adm. and discharge reg's 1884-1933; lunatic return 1884-86; boarded-out children 1916-32; deceased inmates' property inventory 1914-35; DMO's relief book 1913-44; vac. reg. 1899-1925; school attendance reg. 1897-98.
B. Min's 1837-1930; c'tee min's 1837-1930; ledgers 1846-1930; parochial ledgers 1837-1927; treasurer's book 1872-1930; MO's report books 1868-1935; master's report book 1893-96; SAC min's 1877-1903; infant life protection report books 1913-30; sup'an. reg's 1885-1930.
Public Record Office, Kew:
Corres. etc. 1839-1900 (missing 1847-53, 1862-73, 1889-90, 1893-96) [MH 12/6398-410]; staff reg. 1837-1921 [MH 9/2].

Belvoir out-relief union.
B. Min's 1895-1930.

Billesdon [13].
A. Deaths reg. 1836-63; creed reg. 1915-38; punishment book 1854-86; reg. of infants etc. 1904-29; relief order book 1915-26.
B. Min's 1836-1930 (gaps); letter book 1853-61; service reg's 1880-1929.
Public Record Office, Kew:
Corres. etc. 1834-1900 (missing 1843-46, 1851-61, Aug. 1871-73, 1883-85, 1893-96) [MH 12/6413-39]; staff reg. 1837-1921 [MH 9/2].

Bingham [4] (Barkestone, Plungar).
See under Nottinghamshire.

Blaby [12].
A. Adm. and discharge reg's 1911-36; births reg. 1867-1926; deaths reg. 1866-1914; medical cert's for lunatics 1890-1910; death notices of lunatics 1903-37; creed reg's 1899-1938; bathing reg. 1914-

39; punishment book 1914-27; outdoor relief lists 1914-29; vac. reg. 1913-29.
B. Min's 1836-1930; c'tee min's 1908-30; ledgers 1908-30; parochial ledgers 1847-1920; sup'an. ledgers 1896-1930; letter books 1836-1913; report books: chaplain's 1921-26; master's 1905-37.
Public Record Office, Kew:
Corres. etc. 1834-1900 (missing 1843-46, 1851-55, 1862-66) [MH 12/6421-39]; staff reg. 1837-1921 [MH 9/2].

Grantham [5] (Belvoir, Bottesford, Croxton Kerrial, Harston, Knipton, Muston, Redmile).
See under Lincolnshire (Pts. Kesteven).

Hinckley [10] (partly Warws.).
A. Adm. and discharge reg's 1901-36 (index 1890-1933); births reg. 1916-36; deaths reg. 1914-36; porter's adm. and discharge reg. 1916-19; outdoor relief list 1920-23.
B. Min's 1842-1930; ledger 1927-30; alcohol book 1923-24; service reg's 1859-1929.
Public Record Office, Kew:
Corres. etc. 1834-86, 1889-1900 [MH 12/6443-64]; staff reg. 1837-1921 [MH 9/8].

Leicester [11].
See S.J. Page, The mobility of the poor: a case study of Edwardian Leicester', *The Local Historian* **21**.3 (1991) (uses the Charity Organisation Society records, referred to in the Introduction, not PLU records); Kathryn Thompson, 'Apprenticeship and the New Poor Law: a Leicester example', *The Local Historian,* **19**, 2 (May 1989).
A. Adm. and discharge reg's 1879-1973; relief order books 1923-48; reg's of settlements and removals 1900-38; births and deaths reg's 1866-1960; reg's of parochial electors 1894-1914; lunatic list 1851-96; reg. of appr's 1844-1927 (on which article in *The Local Historian* is based); bastardy reg. 1844-87; reg. of deserted children 1911-47; reg. of emigrants 1905-21; pauper index books 1875-1933.
B. Min's 1836-1930; c'tees 1862-1948; ledgers 1836-1930; letter books 1843-1937; form A returns 1848-1946.
Public Record Office, Kew:
Corres. etc. 1834-81, 1883-1900 [MH 12/6468-510]; staff reg. 1837-1921 [MH 9/10].

Loughborough [3] (partly Notts.).
A. Adm. and discharge reg's 1912-18; births and deaths reg's 1838-1900; returns of infant deaths 1890-1916; vac. reg's 1883-1932; papers re. paupers' maintenance 1892-1903.
B. Min's 1837-1930; c'tee min's 1837-39, 1890-1930; ledgers 1875-1930; parochial ledgers 1879-1927; service reg. 1876-1929.
Loughborough Area Library:
'The poor and the English poor laws in the Loughborough union of parishes, 1837-1860.' Memoire presente pour l'obtention de la Maitrise - es - lettres ..., Universite de Nancy, 1972. 259pp. with 2pp. of personal names index.

Leicestershire: Loughborough *continued*

Public Record Office, *Kew:*
Corres. etc. 1834-1900 [MH 12/6523-40]; staff reg.
1837-1921 [MH 9/10].

Lutterworth [15] (partly Warws., Northants.).
A. Births reg's 1847-1932; deaths reg. 1847-1914;
creed reg's 1869-1939; punishment book 1879-
1933; sup'an. reg's 1888-1930.
B. Min's 1835-1930; c'tee min's 1888-1930; ledgers
1836-1930; parochial ledgers 1847-1927; master's
report books 1855-1948; service reg. 1903-29.
Public Record Office, *Kew:*
Corres. etc. 1834-1900 [MH 12/6544-64]; staff reg.
1837-1921 [MH 9/10].

Market Bosworth [9].
A. Births reg. 1915-30; MO's exam. books 1914-40.
B. Min's 1835-1930 (gaps); c'tee min's 1912-30;
ledgers 1918-30; service reg's 1896-1926.
Public Record Office, *Kew:*
Corres. etc. 1834-1900 [MH 12/6566-79]; staff reg.
1837-1921 [MH 9/11].

Market Harborough [16] (partly Northants.).
A. Adm. and discharge reg's 1903-49; births reg.
1837-1914; deaths reg's 1837-1948; creed reg's
1891-1949; reg. of mechanical restraint 1905-45;
punishment book 1914-38; porter's adm. and
discharge books 1908-48; outdoor relief lists 1911-
36

B. Min's 1835-1930; c'tee min's 1912-30; ledger
1928-30; alcohol book 1901-10; sup'an. reg's 1896-
1930.
Public Record Office, *Kew:*
Corres. etc. 1834-1900 [MH 12/ 6581-606]; staff
reg. 1837-1921 [MH 9/11].

Melton Mowbray [6] (partly Notts.).
A. Adm. and discharge reg. 1924-27; births reg's
1836-1913 (gaps); deaths reg. 1836-47; creed reg's
1877-1931; adm. and discharge reg. (children's
home) 1921-28.
B. Min's 1855-58, 1927-30; ledger 1928-30; service
reg's 1883-1930.
Public Record Office, *Kew:*
Corres. etc. 1834-79, 1883-1900 [MH 12/6609-26];
staff reg. 1837-1921 [MH 9/11].

Oakham [14] (Cold Overton, Knossington).
See under Rutland.

Rugby (Westrill and Starmore).
See under Warwickshire.

Shardlow [1] (Breedon on the Hill, Castle
Donington, Diseworth, Hemington, Isley Walton,
Kegworth, Langley Priory, Lockington).
See under Derbyshire.

Uppingham [17] (Blaston, Bringhurst, Drayton, Gt.
Easton, Hallaton, Nevill Holt, Horninghold,
Medbourne, Slawston, Stockerston, Stlike Dry).
See under Rutland.

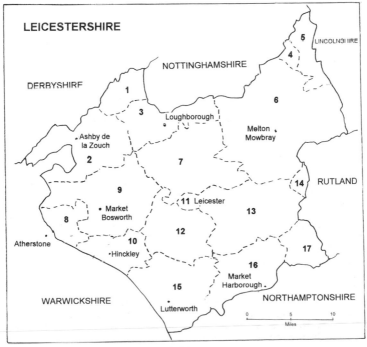

LINCOLNSHIRE

See S. Noble, 'Lincolnshire Poor Law Union records and Family History, 1835-1930', *Lincs. FH*, **5**, 2, Oct. 1985; and J.A. Perkins, 'Unmarried mothers and the Poor Law in Lincolnshire 1800-1850', *Lincs. History and Arch.* **20** (1985) (refers to Lindsey).

Except when shown otherwise, records are at **Lincolnshire Archives Office,** Lincoln.

Boston [12] (Pts. Holland, Pts. Lindsey).
   A. Case papers 1912-29; relief order books (part) 1894-1920; MO's cert's for boarded-out children 1910; adm. and discharge books 1838-9, 1876-1930; porter's adm. and discharge reg's 1885-87, 1922-25; school adm. and discharge reg's: girls 1850-1901, boys 1868-1902; births reg. 1866-79, 1914-42 (indexes 1907-19); deaths reg's 1866-1941; reg. of maternity cases 1910-42; medical relief book 1899-1901; cert. book for pauper lunatics 1890-1928; cert. book for detention of lunatics 1870-1909; reg. of mechanical restraint 1899-1916 (gaps); creed reg's 1901-29; offences and punishment reg. 1880-1941; reg. of addresses of paupers' next of kin or friends 1911-28; reg. of clothes (n.d.) and property reg. 1916-34; out relief book (Kirton) 1906-20 (currently missing); abstracts of out relief, receipts and exp. (Kirton) 1912-29; vac. reg's (Boston 1894-1916, W'h. 1904-42); medical cert's of successful vac's 1928-9; names of chldren needing vac. 1920-28; various rate books, valuation lists etc. 1906-29.
   B. Min's 1836-38, 1841-1930; C'tee min's: Children 1926-30, Finance 1896-1930, House 1919-28, Maintenance and recovery 1927-30, Visiting 1881-97, 1899-1913; ledgers 1836-1930 (gaps); treasurer's ac's 1913-30 (gaps); parochial ledgers 1874-1927; financial statements 1921-30; stat's 1906-09; orders, reg'ns etc. 1836-39; service reg. 1896-1906; wages receipt books 1912-39; contracts of vac. officers 1883-1902, 1905-6, and of DMO's 1898-9, 1905-07; w'h. plans etc. 1904-13; tenders and contracts 1894-1929; corres. 1887-1918; reports books: chaplain 1914-18, master 1914-34, Visiting C'tee 1902-05; master's day book 1889-92 (with summary 1912-18); master's receipts and exp. 1895-1900; detailed w'h. ac's between 1890 and 1940; daily provisions ac's 1928-9; children's homes record of meals 1919-22; RSA ledger 1873-87.
   Public Record Office, Kew:
   Corres. etc. 1834-1900 (missing 1867- Aug. 1871) [MH 12/6629-53]; staff reg. 1837-1921 [MH 9/3].

Bourne [14] (Pts. Kesteven).
   A. Adm. and discharge books 1836-1930 (gaps); births reg's 1866-1930; deaths reg's 1866-1936; creed reg's c.1880-1915 (gaps); punishment book 1914-36; reg. of inmates' friends and kin 1894-1935; appl. and report book (part) 1854-56; DMO relief list 1879-86; vac. reg. (various) 1899-1936; relief list 1836.
   B. Min's 1837-1930 (gaps); House and wood c'tee min's 1902-13; ledgers 1875-77, 1896, 1928-30;

parochial ledgers 1857-59, 1885-89; in letters 1845-1847, 1849-53; PLB letters 1855-58; Assessment C'tee min's 1862-82, 1921-27; master's reports 1842-45; Service reg. 1857-1903, 1907-29.
   Public Record Office, Kew:
   Corres. etc. 1834-1900 (missing 1845-6) [MH 12/6657-75]; staff reg. 1837-1921 [MH 9/3].

Caistor (a Gilbert Union) (Pts. Lindsey).
   A. Possible list of inmates, n.d., in the Guardians' attendance book 1815-32.
   B. Ledgers, treasurer's ac's 1801-37; Juvenile Benefit Society ledger 1822-3; report into exp. 1816; schedule of parishes 1844; Society of Industry c'tee book 1800-1; corres. 1834; House of Industry draft reg'ns c.1802.

Caistor [5] (Pts. Lindsey).
   See C. Rawding, 'The Poor Law Amendment Act 1834-5: case study of Caistor Poor Law Union', *Lincs. Hist. and Arch. Jnl.* **22**, 1987.
   A. Reg. of bastardy orders 1881-1906; MO's relief book (Tealby) 1898-1901.
   B. Min's 1836-1931 (gaps); C'tee min's: Boarding-out 1878-1930, Building and farming 1913-27, Finance 1909-29, House 1913-30, Special 1902-21, Vagrant wards 1899-1928; boarding-out receipt and exp. ac's 1910-29; reports of House C'tee 1916-30; master's reports 1925-27; reg. of officers etc. 1897-1930.
   North East Lincolnshire Archives, Grimsby:
   A. Vac. reg. (Grimsby district) 1875-6 [309/1].
   Public Record Office, Kew:
   Corres. etc. 1847-1900 (missing 1856-58, 1889, 1893-4) [MH 12/6677-706]; staff reg. 1837-1921 [MH 9/4].
   See also under Grimsby (formed 1890 from Caistor).

Doncaster (Pts. Lindsey: Misson).
   See under Yorkshire West Riding.

Gainsborough [4] (Pts. Lindsey) (partly Notts.).
   A. Adm. and discharge books 1889-1935 (gaps) (casuals 1913-23, 1927-30); births reg. 1914-22; baptisms reg. 1888-1961; deaths reg's 1866-1935; reg. of mental defectives seen by Visiting C'tee 1907-41; notices to coroner on deaths of lunatics 1901-33; creed reg's 1879-1930 (gaps; partly indexed); punishment book 1903-48; reg. of owners of voting proxies 1889.
   B. Min's 1843-54, 1859-1930; C'tee min's: Boarding-out 1911-30, House 1914-16, Assessment 1862-1916, SAC 1877-89, 1897-1903; ledgers 1837-1930 (gaps); treasurer's ac's 1912-24; parochial ledgers 1848-56, 1867-1927; financial statements 1898-9, 1902-05; w'h. plans etc. c.1837-1916; letter books 1890-1918; w'h. reg'ns 1920's; wages books 1906-35; reg. of salaries 1928-30; chaplain's reports 1913-47; master's weekly reports 1902-13, 1917-21; matron's reports 1926-34; MO's reports 1913-29; master's receipts and exp. ac's 1909-32; detailed w'h. ac's between 1910 and 1934; returns of births (Misterton) 1878-81; letter book (assessment) 1884-93; min's of election of school board 1871-96; SAC corres. 1890's; infant life protection inspector's reports 1898-1908.

32

Lincolnshire: Gainsborough *continued*
Public Record Office, Kew:
Corres. etc. 1839-1899 (missing 1851-54, 1862-1866, 1874-5, 1881-84, 1887-97) [MH 12/6707-17]; staff reg. 1837-1921 [MH 9/7].

Glanford Brigg [3] (Pts. Lindsey).
A. Births reg. 1914-44; reg. of inmates c.1928-37.
B. Min's 1920-30; C'tee min's: Boarding-out 1912-1930, others 1898-1930; service reg. 1910-30.
Public Record Office, Kew:
Corres. etc. 1836-1900 (missing 1836-46, 1851-1868, Aug. 1871-1876, 1879-89, 1893-96) [MH 12/6718-23]; staff reg. 1837-1921 [MH 9/7].

Goole [1] (Pts. Lindsey: Garthorpe, Luddington).
See under Yorkshire West Riding.

Grantham [13] (Pts. Kesteven) (partly Leics.).
A. Vac. reg. (Burton Coggles) 1899-1930.
B. Min's 1863-1930; C'tee min's: House 1914-30, Finance and Relief 1927-29, Women's 1928-30, Boarding-out 1927-30, Visiting and contracts 1898-1914; ledgers 1923-26, 1929-30; out-relief minutes 1895-1930 (gaps); service reg. 1862-1930.
Public Record Office, Kew:
Corres. etc. 1835- Apr. 1890 (missing 1835-66, 1869-77, 1879-80, 1883-4) [MH 12/6725-34]; staff reg. 1837-1921 [MH 9/7].

Grimsby (Pts Lindsey, formed 1890 out of **Caistor**).
North East Lincolnshire Archives (formerly South Humberside), Grimsby:
A. Relief lists 1920-28; indoor relief lists 1929-30.
B. Min's 1890-1930; C'tee min's: SAC 1890-97, Finance 1907-20, House 1907-19, Maintenance and recovery 1906-16, Boarding-out 1905-18, Out-relief 1915-19, Nursing 1929-30, General office 1929-30, others 1890-98; corres. 1890-1929; various publications, C20; acts and orders 1844-90.
Public Record Office, Kew:
No papers in MH 12, staff reg. 1890-1921 [MH 9/7].

Grimsby Brighowgate Children's Home.
North East Lincolnshire Archives, Grimsby:
A. Adm. and discharges 1920-59 (closed); reg. of servants and appr's 1929-37.
B. Superintendent's day books 1920-59 (with summaries); superintendent's journals 1920-53; requisition books 1920-52; receipt and exp. books 1919-50; provisions ac's books 1920-55; provisions receipt and consumption books 1920-55 (with summaries).

Grimsby Scartho Road.
North East Lincolshire Archives, Grimsby:
A. Births reg's 1895-1903, 1914-53; deaths reg's 1894-56; creed reg's 1910-51 (closed 75 years); vac. reg. 1927-51; reg. of mechanical restraint 1908-50.
B. Master's report books 1919-29; Inspector of Nuisances' journal 1895-97; salaries reg. 1913-48; wage books 1912-15, 1921-42; inventory books c.1927-40; corres. etc. 1890-1929.

Holbeach [16] (Pts. Holland) (partly Norfolk).
A. Adm. and discharge books 1904-5, 1913-16, 1929-33; deaths reg. 1914-36; lunatic exam. book 1870-93.
B. Min's 1835-1930; ledgers 1836-42, 1844-1930; treasurer's ac's 1926-30; parochial ledgers 1836, 1848-67, 1878-1912; non-resident and non-settled poor ledger 1845-75; PLC orders etc. 1837-44, 1848-51, 1888-90; letter books, 1865-6, 1870-73, 1925-6; Assessment C'tee min's 1862-90; RSA min's 1872-96; RSA ledgers 1874-94; SAC ledger 1878-97; service reg. 1896-1906.
Public Record Office, Kew:
No papers in MH 12; staff reg. 1837-1921 [MH 9/8].

Horncastle [8] (Pts. Lindsey).
See C.L. Anderson, 'How the poor of Horncastle were treated', *Lincs. Hist and Arch N/L*, **48-60**, 1986.
B. Min's 1837-1925; C'tee min's: Building 1837-41, General Purposes 1898-1930, Vac. 1891-1914, Assessment 1862-90, RSA 1891-1914; collector's monthly statements 1914-5; reg's of officers etc. 1903 30; officers' salaries etc. 1903-10; wages 1921-2, 1927-29; letter book 1916-18.
Lincoln Central Reference Library:
'An Account of the Persons assessed to the Poor Rate in the Parish of Horncastle ... 1836' (poll for church rates).
Public Record Office, Kew:
No papers in MH 12; staff reg. 1837-1921 [MH 9/9].

Lincoln [6] (Pts. Kesteven, Pts. Lindsey).
A. Adm. and discharge books 1839-43, 1871-1931 (gaps); porter's adm. and discharge book 1922-3; baptisms reg. 1827-62, 1900-45; births reg. 1911-1949; burials reg's 1828-45, 1858-99; deaths reg's 1911 44; creed reg's 1876-1933 (gaps); inmates' property reg. 1914-33; adm. and discharge reg. (Children's Home) 1897-1920, vac. reg's (various) 1911-31.
B. Min's 1836-1930; C'tee min's: Assessment 1862-1933, Boarding-out 1897-1930, Building 1899-1902, 1910-30, Children's Homes 1900-06, 1914-30, Special Unemployment 1924-28, Unemployment (finance) 1923-30, Visitors (Ladies) 1907-38; letter book 1836-43; master's reports 1877-1931 (gaps; half yearly 1915-40); nurses' reports 1914-41; returns of births and vac. (various) 1883-1909.
Lincoln Central Reference Library:
A. Parochial lists of indoor and outdoor paupers, ac's (printed) 1882.
B. House of Industry ac's (printed) 1825-36.
Public Record Office, Kew:
Corres. etc. 1836-94 (missing 1836-76, 1879-89, 1892) [MH 12/6732-34]; staff reg. 1837-1921 [MH 9/10].

Louth [7] (Pts. Lindsey).
A. Adm. and discharge books 1872-1934 (gaps) (casuals 1906-08, 1929-30); births reg's c.1847-65, 1910-36; deaths reg. 1837-66, 1914-36; creed reg's 1869-1930 (gaps); reg. of lunatics in w'h. 1895-1905.

Lincolnshire: Louth *continued*

B. Min's 1837-64, 1866-1930; C'tee min's: Boarding-out 1906-30, Diseases prevention 1866-74, Finance 1903-12, House 1925-29, RSA 1872-88, SAC 1885-93, 1896-1902, Scattered Homes 1913-25; ledger 1853-55; treasurer's ac's 1923-28; letter book 1861-65; deeds etc. re. property C19; House c'tee reports 1925-29; DMO ledger (Hainton) 1875-85; returns of deaths of infants 1889-94; receipt book for voluntary school rate (Alvingham) 1891; salaries reg. 1923-30; reg. of assistant overseers 1926.

Public Record Office, Kew:
Corres. etc. 1834-1900 (missing 1840-42, 1875-6, 1889-90, 1895-6) [MH 12/6738-61]; staff reg. 1837-1921 [MH 9/10].

Newark [10] (Pts. Lindsey: Allington, Barkston, Bassingham, Beckingham, Long Bennington, Bennington Grange (1861-1930), Brant Broughton, Carlton le Moorland, Caythorpe, Claypole, Dry Doddington, Fenton, Flawford (1866-84), Foston, Fulbeck, Hougham, Marston, Norton Disney, North Scarle, Sedgebrook, Stapleford, Stragglethorpe, Stubton, Swinderby, Syston, Thurlby, Westborough).
See under Nottinghamshire.

Peterborough [18] (Pts. Holland: Crowland).
See under Northamptonshire.

Sleaford [11] (Pts. Kesteven).
A. Adm. and discharge books 1896-1939; porter's adm. and discharge books 1922-35; births reg. 1914-29; creed reg. 1904-40; punishment book (Slea View) 1853-1914; offences and punishment book 1914-48; inmates' exam. book 1929-48; reg. of friends c.1898-c1930; vac. reg. (Wilsford) 1899-1929; returns of pauper lunatics 1867-90; inmates' exam. book 1929-48.
B. Min's 1836-1930; C'tee min's: Boarding-out 1928-9, House 1914-22, 1926-28; ledgers 1838-40, 1927-30; letter book 1837; PLC orders 1836-47.

Public Record Office, Kew:
Corres. etc. 1834-1900 (missing 1848-55, 1867-72) [MH 12/6763-80]; staff reg. 1837-1921 [MH 9/15].

Spalding [15] (Pts. Holland, Pts. Kesteven).
A. Adm. and discharge books 1913-16, 1924-28; Relief order book 1911-13, 1916-19; indoor relief list 1928-9; reg. of lunatics 1914-48 (closed); reg. of mechanical restraint 1899-1943 (closed); creed reg. 1914-36; inmates' complaint and appl. book 1914-38; punishment book 1862-1929; appl. and report book 1926-7; out relief lists (Gosberton 1912-27, Spalding 1914-16, 1919-30); relief book 1928-30.
B. Min's 1835-1930; C'tee min's: Assessment 1863-1926, RSA 1872-94; ledgers 1836-1931; treasurer's ac's 1918-30; parochial ledger 1859-1919 (gaps); non-resident and non-settled poor ledgers 1845-48, 1898-1916; letter books 1871-1928 (gaps); inventory 1922; dietaries etc. c.1900; RSA letter book 1873-97; RSA ledger 1891-93;

parochial ledger (RSA) 1866-89, 1892-95; service reg. etc. 1886-1912; sup'an. reg. etc. 1886-1903.

Public Record Office, Kew:
Corres. etc. 1838-1900 (missing 1864-66, 1883-88, July 1890 - Apr. 1895) [MH 12/6781-95]; staff reg. 1837-1921 [MH 9/16].

Spilsby [9] (Pts. Lindsey).
B. Min's 1837-72, 1876-1930; C'tee min's: Assessment 1862-1927, Building 1837-42, Boarding-out 1910-30, Finance 1928-30, House 1838-42, 1916-30, SAC 1890-1903; letter book 1905-07; service reg. 1904-30.

Public Record Office, Kew:
Corres. etc. 1839-1900 (missing 1847-57) [MH 12/6797-816]; staff reg. 1837-1921 [MH 9/16].

Stamford [17] (Pts. Kesteven) (partly Northants. (1835-89), Soke of Peterborough).
A. Adm. and discharge book 1920-25; vac. reg. (Stamford) 1925-30.
B. Min's 1835-88, 1904-30; Assessment C'tee min's 1914-26; ledgers 1915-27; treasurer's ledger 1928-30; parochial ledgers 1911-27; visitors' and Visiting C'tee reports 1870-1914; reg. of officers etc. 1893-1916, 1920-30.

Public Record Office, Kew:
Corres. etc. 1834-1900 [MH 12/6820-38]; staff reg. 1837-1921 [MH 9/16].

Thorne [2] (Pts. Lindsey: Althorpe, Amcotts, Belton, Crowle, Eastoft, Epworth, Keadby, Wroot).
See under Yorkshire West Riding.

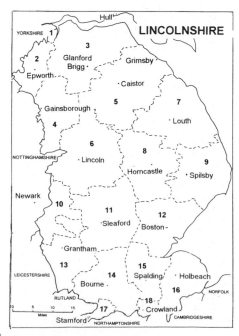

34

NORTHAMPTONSHIRE

The PLU in which each parish lay is shown in the Northamptonshire volume of the *National Index of Parish Registers*, **8**, 2 (Society of Genealogists, 1992).

Unless shown otherwise, records are at **Northamptonshire Record Office, Northampton.**

Banbury [15] (Appletree, Aston le Walls, Lower and Upper Boddington, Chalcombe, Edgcote, Grimsbury (Banbury), Middleton Cheney, Chipping Warden, Warkworth).
See under Oxfordshire.

Brackley [16] (partly in Oxon., Bucks.).
A: Adm. and discharge reg's 1916-30 (vagrants 1914-30); indoor relief lists 1912-27 (with statement 1910-14 and abstract 1908-31); MO's report books 1913-32; lunatics: medical cert's 1899-1907, annual returns 1896-1904, quarterly lists 1892-1912; births reg. 1910-32; deaths reg. 1910-31, reg. of children retained 1911-16; reg's of clothes, n.d.; creed reg's 1890-1934 (incl. names of relatives); relief order books 1848-1930 (gaps); appl. and report books 1837-42, 1917-24; outdoor relief lists and abstracts 1835-42, 1881-1924 (gaps); reg. of persons receiving reward for children 1909-29 (and receipts 1928-9); collector's receipts and exp. 1921-27.
B. Min's 1835-1906, 1914-30 (rough 1837-1911), C'tee min's: Assessment 1862-92, 1901-04, SAC 1077-1907, in-letters 1897-1907, 1927; out-letters 1835-1900, 1909-13, appointment of overseers, MO's 1888-1914; bonds 1849-75; parochial ledgers 1848-1927 (gaps) and balance sheets 1856-81; ledgers 1848-1929; treasurer's ledgers 1835-48; financial statements 1872, 1889-1905, 1919-30; rate estimates 1872-78 and precept book 1928; collector's monthly statements 1859-82, 1896-1913, 1919-30; loan ac's 1836-45; vouchers 1843-80, 1929-30; magistrates' licences 1908-29; salaries ac's 1920-30; petty cash vouchers 1872; charges for building w'h. 1836-7; sale of land 1835, 1848-54; drainage plan 1888; building contract 1835-6; master's: report and journal 1909-11, 1916-29, day book and summary 1918-30, receipts and exp. 1907-34, petty cash 1899-1930, reports and estimates 1915-33; tenders 1906-16, 1920-36; dietary book 1914-19; wages books 1919-28; pauper description or classification 1835, 1840, 1848-1910 (gaps); porter's books 1913-30; provisions etc. 1836-39, 1910-30 (detailed ac's of clothing, extras etc.); relieving officer's receipts and exp. (Sulgrave 1836-41, 1917-30); outdoor relief and exp. (Brackley 1836-41, 1845-48); return of outdoor paupers 1904-20 (gaps); papers re. assisted emigration to Canada 1853-4; boarded-out pay book 1912-30; casuals' provisions 1927; PLC, LGB orders etc. 1835-51, 1870-74; vac. contracts 1840-63.
Public Record Office, *Kew:*
Corres. etc. 1835-1900 [MH 12/8671-88]; staff reg. 1837-1921 [MH 9/3].

Brixworth [10].
A. Collector's receipt and exp. book 1907-30; maintenance by relatives 1898-1908; adm. and discharge orders 1840, 1910-35; punishment book 1889-1934; indoor relief list 1909-10; leave of absence books 1901-16; MO exam. books 1914-34; tuberculosis reg. 1912-23; reg. of lunatics 1888-90; medical cert's (lunatics) 1853-63; births reg. 1837-1920; deaths reg. 1837-1934; creed reg's 1880-1920; relief order books (part) 1897-1930; appl. and report books 1838-46, 1906-30 (part, gaps); outdoor relief lists 1838-45, 1914-30 (part, gaps); casuals adm. and discharge book 1910-14; vac. reg's 1853-56, 1882-95; school attendance and fees reg. 1875-77; cause of deaths 1924-31.
B. Min's 1835-1923, 1929-30; House C'tee min's 1886-1914, 1928-30 (reports 1914-28); letter books 1835-41, 1883-1915; weekly returns 1904-30; contract books 1902-28; ledgers (incl. parochial and non-settled poor) 1848-1916 (gaps); treasurer's ledger 1837-48; financial statements 1900-15; treasurer's book 1903-08; reg. of securities 1900-13; w'h. plans 1859; inventory book 1919; master's: report and journal 1908-10, 1913-29, day books 1910-31, receipts and exp. 1899-1934, requisition books 1908-30, letter books 1917, 1923; matron's report book 1914-19; wages 1912-31; porter's books 1910-30; visitors' book 1893-97, 1909-14; dietaries 1901, 1911-21, provisions, extras etc. 1905-31; MO's reports 1901-14, 1923; Visiting C'tee books 1892-1934; reports on children, school 1906-27 (gaps); nurses' report books 1904-30; chaplain's report book 1904-34; corres. (disposal of bodies under Anatomy Act) 1930; relieving officer's receipt and exp. books 1837-41, 1905-28 (part, gaps); summary of paupers 1910-20; payment for children 1912-30.
Public Record Office, *Kew:*
Corres. etc. 1835-1900 [MH 12/8689-707]; staff reg. 1837-1921 [MH 9/3].

Daventry [12].
A. Valuation lists 1883-1905 (gaps); rate books 1905-21 (gaps); indoor relief lists 1879-1930 (gaps); inmates' relatives c.1920; persons maintained elsewhere c.1928; porter's adm. and discharge books 1894-1936 (gaps); MO's exam. book 1922-35; w'h. medical relief book 1912-3; lunatics: reg. 1896-1901, returns 1918-30; persons suffering from tuberculosis 1913-40; creed reg's c.1902-34; relief order books 1909-28; outdoor relief lists and abstracts 1899-1916; boarded-out relief lists 1911-27; medical exam. of children 1925-36; reg. of children retained medically 1924-26; relief lists (children) 1912-25; children in Braunston Cottage Home 1901-34; adm. and discharge books 1901-28 (vagrants 1927-8); deaths reg. 1919, 1922; reg. of appl's by casuals 1925-41; reg's of persons receiving children 1909-30.
B. Min's 1836-55, 1874-1930; C'tee min's: Boarding-out 1910-26, Cottage Homes 1901-30, Finance 1914-30, Permanent Visiting 1910-30, SAC 1877-1903; Boarding out C'tee reports and corres.

1920-28; Cottage Home corres. 1921-30; Permanent Visiting C'tee corres. 1921-30; scale of out-relief 1922; in-letters (and LGB) 1909-30; out-letters 1879-1929 (gaps); Guardians' declarations of office 1895-1928; list of Guardians and paid officers 1881-1915; appl's for posts 1914-30; weekly returns 1909-25; contracts 1923-4; sup'an. corres. 1920-30; ledgers 1885-1928; parochial ledgers 1883-1927; estimates and statements etc. 1920's; financial statements 1895-1930; corres. etc. on rates, C20; parish collectors' monthly statements 1883, 1918-27 (gaps); treasurer's books 1903-30; reg. of securities 1903-4; treasurer's ac's books 1918-29; vouchers etc. 1882-3, 1923-30; poor rate returns 1900-29; salaries 1887-1930 (gaps); plans etc. 1836-1914 (gaps); master's: day books 1911-14, 1920-28, requisition, cash books etc. 1914-40, order book 1883, 1924, receipt and exp. book 1901-13; reports of cases adm'd without orders 1914-30; visitors' book 1922-32; stores, clothing etc. 1902-36 (gaps); vac. returns 1899-1930; out-relief ac's 1925-29; relief to non-settled poor 1929; boarded-out receipt and exp. book 1910-27; reports on boarded-out children 1919-20, 1923-4; reception of children for nursing 1909-29; indoor poor weekly returns 1910-31; MO's reports 1905-13; provisions etc. 1906-29; PLC, LGB, MoH orders etc. 1835, 1921-30.

Public Record Office, Kew:
Corres. etc. 1838-1900 [MH 12/8711-29]; staff reg. 1837-1921 [MH 9/6].

Hardingstone [14].

A. Valuation lists 1871, 1874, 1892, 1895 (part); overseers' receipts and exp. (part) 1903-27; collector's receipts and exp. 1873-76, 1922-28 (part); adm. and discharge books 1901-25 (casuals 1907-25); indoor relief lists 1836-48, 1859-1925 (gaps); reg. of relatives' addresses 1907; property reg. 1914-24; w'h. medical relief book 1904-23; lunatics: exam. book 1875-1915, cert's 1903, orders 1905-6; births reg. 1837-87, 1915-22; deaths reg. 1836-1925 (gaps); monthly list of deaths 1872-1907; DMO relief books 1907-22 (part); creed reg. 1900-15; outdoor relief order books 1912-17; appl. and report books 1871-1926 (gaps); outdoor relief lists 1836-1925 (gaps, with abstracts 1893-1930); appl's for unemployment relief 1925-6; reg. of successful vac's 1853-73; vac. reg's 1871-1905 (part); vac. cert's 1867-98; lists of children not yet vac'd 1899, 1923; school attendance reg. (Wootton) 1887-89.

B. Min's 1835-1914; out-letters 1866-96; ag'mts re. poor rate 1924-26; ledgers 1848-1930; parochial ledgers 1853-1914 (earliest damaged; abstracts 1915-27); treasurer's ledgers 1835-48; financial statements 1905-20; rate books (expenses) 1925-6; collector's monthly statements 1920-27 (part); treasurer's receipts and exp. 1898-1905, 1911-24; collector's receipt book 1922-4; rate receipt book 1926-7; boarded-out receipts 1912, 1922; w'h. inventory book 1867-1915; master's: report books and journals 1911-25, day book and summary 1908-

25, receipts and exp. 1901-25; petty cash 1899-1918; articles needed in w'h. 1908-25; porter's book 1916-23; visitors' book 1908-14; Lady Visitors' book 1893-1925; various provisions books, ac's etc. between 1898 and 1925; medical health reports 1899-1917; MO's report book 1924-5; Visiting C'tee books (lunatics) 1887-1924; chaplain's report books 1904-25; relieving officer's receipt and exp. book 1905-25 (gaps) and vouchers 1916-28; children report book 1921-27; vac. officer's report book 1899-1903; SAC min's 1877-1903; corres. 1873-1911.

Public Record Office, Kew:
Corres. etc. 1835-1900 [MH 12/8731-46]; staff reg. 1837-1921 [MH 9/8].

Kettering [6].

B.L. = Burton Latimer; K. = Kettering; R. = Rothwell.

A. Overseers' receipts and exp. books (part) 1910-27; collector's receipt and exp. books: K. 1899-1930, B.L. 1911-30 (gaps); adm. and discharge reg's 1907-8, 1911-31 (casuals 1920-29); notices of births and deaths 1923, 1927-9; indoor relief list 1915-6; addresses of paupers' friends 1906-28 (gaps); punishment book 1886-1911, 1920-28; bathing reg. 1924-37; reg. of aliens 1916-18; MO's exam. books (lunatics) 1924-48; lists of lunatics 1921-30; births reg. 1893-1912; deaths reg. 1893-1914; notices of deaths 1927-29; outdoor relief order books: K. 1915-30, R. 1925-30, B.L. 1911-16, 1923-30; appl. and report books: B.L. 1912-30 (gaps), K. 1909-30, R. 1909-30; outdoor relief lists: B.L. 1913-30 (abstract 1899-1917), K. 1848-53, 1909-30, R. 1909-16 (abstract 1900-17), Corby and R. 1848-51; reg. of persons chargeable 1918; settlement orders 1857-80; boarding-out relief list 1915-30; MO's exam. of children 1924-26; addresses of military officers 1890; casuals refused or discharged 1916.

B. Min's 1836-39, 1863-1930; C'tee min's: Boarding-out 1890-1914, 1924-30, House 1914-18 (reports 1915-20), Ladies 1914-29, Relief 1887-89; out-letters 1913-19; Guardians' declarations of acceptance 1907-28 and attendance reg. 1911-30; returns 1919-30; ledgers 1870-1930; parochial ledgers 1865-1927 (gaps); treasurer's ledger 1917-19; financial statements 1911-30; treasurer's book 1919-30; collector's ledgers: K. 1907-30, B.L. 1922-29; ac's book 1891-98; vouchers etc. 1913-33; Guardians' luncheon ac's 1920-25; sales 1923-27; estimates 1928-32; inventory 1904-12; master's: report and journal 1874-89, day book 1914-29 (summary 1899-1914, 1921-27), receipt and exp. book 1909-27, corres. 1922, 1927-29; requisition books 1927-29; reg. of supply contracts 1911; wages book 1913-29; delivery note books 1927-29; daily numbers relieved 1916-27; porter's book 1922-29; visitors' book (lunatics) 1863-79, 1916-25; dietaries 1908, 1920-29; stores, provisions etc. 1889-90, 1918-29; w'h. medical relief book 1923-25; County Council repayments (lunatics) 1907-10; relieving officer's receipts and exp.: B.L. 1912-30, K. 1908-30, R. 1909-23; boarding-out commission statement 1926-30; vagrants' provision and

Northamptonshire: Kettering *continued*

consumption 1914-20; LGB orders etc. 1909, 1914; vac. papers 1915-27.
Public Record Office, Kew:
Corres. etc. 1835-1900 [MH 12/8749-72]; staff reg. 1837-1921 [MH 9/9].

Lutterworth [8] (Welford).
See under Leicestershire.

Market Harborough [5] (Arthingworth, Ashley, Little Bowden, Brampton Ash, Braybrooke, Clipston, Dingley, East Frandon, Hothorpe, Kelmarsh, Marston Trussel, Gt. Oxendon, Sibbertoft, Stoke Albany, Sulby, Sutton Bassett, Thorpe Lubenham (from 1863), Welford (from 1894), Weston by Welland, Wilbarston).
See under Leicestershire.

Newport Pagnall (Hanslope).
See under Buckinghamshire.

Northampton [13].
A. Adm and discharge books 1837-39, 1877-8, 1901-33; births reg's 1837-1915; deaths reg's 1837-70, 1889-1915; DMO's relief book 1896-1900; relief orders book 1907-30; appl. and report books (part) 1900-03; outdoor relief lists (part) 1901-03; indoor and outdoor weekly reg's 1874-78, 1889-91; valuation lists (part) 1911-14.
B. Guardians: min's 1850-60, motion book 1836-1930, declarations 1907-28, reg of attendance 1916-30; C'tee min's: Boarding-out 1911-18, House 1914-26, Visiting 1900-13, Ladies 1893-1929, Overseers 1900-07; ledgers 1835-42, 1848-1930 (gaps); parochial ledger 1907-23; non-settled poor ledger 1874-1909; master's House C'tee book 1929-32.
Northampton Central Library:
B. Min's 1835-6, 1839-44; first Union report; ac's 1889, 1891-2, 1894; newscutting reports of meetings 1902-06.
Public Record Office, *Kew:*
Corres. etc. 1835-1900 [MH 12/8780-801]; staff reg. 1837-1921 [MH 9/12].

Oundle [4] (partly in Hunts.).
A. Overseers' books of receipts and exp. 1905-16, 1921-26; collector's receipts and exp. 1893-1902, 1906-30; adm. and discharge books 1836-1926 (gaps); indoor relief lists 1892-1928; offence book 1842-49; punishment books 1870-1915; lunatics: reg's 1876-1929, medical cert's 1884-97, returns 1854-1930; births reg. 1877-1913 (counterfoils 1920-1); deaths reg's 1848-1914; DMO relief: list 1891-97, book 1913-17; creed reg's 1869-89, 1896-1914; outdoor relief order books 1891-1930; appl. and report books 1912-24 (gaps); outdoor relief lists 1841-46, 1891-1925 (gaps; abstracts 1881-1928); undertakings by foster parents 1883-88, 1890-94, 1918-22; reg. of persons caring for infants 1911-29; weekly payments to foster parents 1911-26; reg. of chargeability 1917; reg's of births and vac. dates 1884-1920 (and vac's, Fotheringhay, 1884-93, 1899-

1902, Barnwell 1901-14); valuation lists (part) 1875-86.
B. Min's 1835-1930; c'tee attendance books 1887-1930 (gaps); C'tee min's: Boarding-out 1910-23, Assessment 1881-86, 1895-97; Visitors: appointments 1923-4, reports 1912-23; House C'tee reports 1927-48; in-letters 1911-28; out-letters 1878-1931; weekly returns 1887-1930 (gaps); staff reg. 1883-1931; ledgers 1848-1930; parochial ledgers 1848-66, 1873-1927; treasurer's ledgers 1836-47; financial statements 1890-1930; loan ac's 1899-1923, 1927-8; corres. etc. re. defectives 1917-8; collector's monthly statements 1916-27; treasurer's books 1868-1930 (gaps); vouchers 1915-30; poor rate etc. returns 1864-1930; salaries 1909-29; advert's for tenders, staff etc. 1871-83; inventory books 1895, 1903-28; master's: report books 1842-1928 (missing 1902), day books 1906-29 (summary 1885-1922); petty cash book 1880-1930; porter's book 1913-30; visitors' books 1836-38, 1870-1914; misc., extras ac's etc. 1877-1938; reg. of places licensed for marriages and appointments of registrars 1913-24; chaplain's report books 1855-1920; relieving officer's: notebook 1927-8, receipt and exp. 1893-1923 (gaps); teacher's reports 1916-23; vagrants' papers 1891-1925; corres. between 1884 and 1918; vac.: contracts 1889-1917, returns 1878-1930, officers' report books (part) 1873-98; SAC byelaws, letters, reg. of proceedings between 1877 and 1896; King's Cliffe School Board min's 1897-1903, and treasurer's book 1876-88, assessment corres. 1881-86, 1895-97; assessment reports 1864-1922.
Public Record Office, Kew:
Corres. etc. 1835-1900 [MH 12/8809-26]; staff reg. 1837-1921 [MH 9/12]

Peterborough [2] (partly in Cambridgeshire, Isle of Ely, Lincs. (Pts. Lind.), Hunts.).
Northamptonshire Record Office, Northampton:
A. Collector's receipt and exp. book 1896-1905; adm. and discharge books 1836-1930 (abstract 1919-31) (casuals 1914-30); indoor relief list 1915-20; reg. of friends and relatives c.1914, c.1920, c.1925, c.1930; porter's adm. and discharge books 1918-31; appl's and complaints 1914-30; MO's exam. books 1914-42; reg. of lunatics 1898-1910; notification to coroner of deaths of lunatics 1914-41; reg. of mechanical restraint 1890-1943; births reg's 1836-1945; deaths reg's 1836-1931; maternity reg. 1912-41; creed reg's c.1915, c.1920, 1929-45; non-resident and non-settled poor c.1912; MO's exam. of children 1914-23; appr. indentures 1869-1915; deaf and dumb children placed out 1898; returns of births and vac's (Crowland 1886-1905, Peterborough 1904 18, Stilton 1895-1912, Thorney 1882-1905.
B. Min's 1835-1930; C'tee min's: W'h. 1904-30, Boarding-out 1910-30, SAC 1877-1903, General 1897-1928; out letters 1882-1901; weekly returns 1914-21; ledgers 1836-1930; parochial ledgers 1848-1930; treasurer's ledgers 1917-28; financial statements 1878-1930; valuation list summary 1863-99; treasurer's book 1927-30; contributors' and

37

Northamptonshire: Peterborough *continued*

collectors' ledgers (various) 1924-38; inventory book
c.1929; boiler exam. 1923-30; master's requisition
book 1916-30, report book and journal 1895-1932,
day book 1912-31 (summary 1908-39), receipts and
exp. 1916-31, half-yearly reports 1914-34; servants'
reg. 1850-91; monthly wages book 1926-28;
invoices 1928-33; House C'tee submissions 1914-
30; daily provisions consumption 1895-6, 1917-30;
weekly provisions issued 1917-30; provisions receipt
and consumption 1908, 1915-30 (with ac's 1913-30);
detailed w'h. ac's, various, between 1891 and 1930;
MO report books 1914-32; MO's record 1929-38;
store ac's 1898-1919; PLC/LGB orders etc. 1836-98.
Northampton Central Library:
B. Min's 1835-6, 1839-44; printed statements of
ac's 1889, 1891-2, 1894; newspaper reports of
meetings 1902-06.
Cambridgeshire Record Office, Cambridge.
B. Valuation lists; North Stanground 1920, Thorney
1921-23.
Public Record Office, Kew:
Corres. etc. 1835-1900 [MH 12/8828-54]; staff reg.
1837-1921 [MH 9/13].

Potterspury [18] (partly in Bucks.).
Buckinghamshire Record Office, Aylesbury:
B. Min's 1840-1930; SAC min's 1887-1896.
Northamptonshire Record Office, Northampton.
B. Weekly returns 1926-30.
Public Record Office, Kew:
Corres. etc. 1835-1900 [MH 12/16727-40]; staff
reg. 1837-1921 [MH 9/13].

Rugby [9] (Barby, Claycoton, Crick, Elkington,
Kilsby, Lilbourne, Stanford, Yelvertoft).
See under Warwickshire.

Southam (Stoneton).
See under Warwickshire.

Stamford [1] (Ashton (to 1877), Bainton, Barnack,
Collyweston, Duddington, Easton on the Hill,
Pilsgate (to 1887), St. Martin Without (from 1894),
Southorpe, Stamford Baron, Thornhaugh, Ufford,
Wansford, Wittering, Wothorpe).
See under Lincolnshire (Pts. Kesteven).

Thrapston [7] (partly in Hunts.).
A. Rate book 1927; reg. of persons excepted from
Unemployment Insurance 1921-27; adm. and
discharge books 1901-33 (vagrants 1903-31); indoor
relief lists 1899-1923 (gaps; abstracts 1904-15);
addresses of paupers' friends 1884-1932; visitors'
books 1881-87, 1898-1933; reg. of inmates' property
1926-33; bathing reg. 1916-26; w'h. medical relief
books 1902-14; lunatics: w'h. reg. 1905-29, appl's
for detention 1903-28, medical cert's 1875-1929;
births reg's 1839-1932; deaths reg's 1837-1933;
maternity reg. 1912-32; creed reg. 1914-32 (indexed
from 1916); outdoor relief order book 1923-30;
settlement orders 1908-33; medical exam. of
children 1921-33; reg. of vagrants' appl's refused
1925-29; reg. of purveyors of milk 1922-26.

B. Min's 1835-1930 (gaps); C'tee min's: Boarding-
out 1911-30, House 1914-30, SAC 1877-1903; in-
letters 1913-30; out-letters 1887-1930; ledgers
1892-95, 1903-26; financial statements 1924-30;
rating notices 1926; parish collectors' monthly
statements (part) 1913-27; treasurer's books,
vouchers etc. 1925-30; w'h. inventories 1888-1933;
master's: journal and report books 1891-1927
(gaps), half-yearly report 1921-27, day books 1900-
28 (summary 1893-1932), receipt and exp. books
1880-1933; matron's report book 1914-16; articles
required in w'h. 1917-20; contracts 1926-30; wages
1921-30; special provisions and stimulants 1921-26;
daily consumption books 1914-5, 1921-30; extras for
females 1905-31; clothing etc. ac's between 1884
and 1933; MoH report books 1901-33 and reports
1914-29; Visiting C'tee (lunatics) book 1888-1918;
nurses' reports books 1916-30; infirmary dietaries
1918; chaplain's report books 1880-1933; Boarding-
out C'tee visitors' weekly payment book 1919-29;
wood ac's 1888-1936; PLB order 1836; vac.
contracts 1888-1922.
Public Record Office, Kew:
Corres. etc. 1835-1900 [MH 12/8861-77]; staff reg.
1837-1921 [MH 9/17].

Towcester [17].
Bl. = Blakesley; T. = Towcester.
A. Valuation lists (part) between 1899 and 1905;
contribution vouchers for maintenance 1910-16;
adm. and discharge books 1901-05, 1922-29
(abstract 1916-23) (vagrants 1923-4, 1927-30);
indoor relief lists 1883-1928 (gaps; abstract 1908-
16); punishment book 1899-1933 (children 1916-21);
inmates medical exam. book 1925-31 (children
1915-28); reg. of lunatics 1892-1922; deaths reg.
1837-1930; creed reg. c.1914-30; out-relief order
books 1924-29; appl. and report books: Bl. 1893-
1911 (gaps), Bl. and T. 1894-1912 (gaps), T. 1896-
1904, 1913-29; and lists 1912-3; outdoor relief lists:
Bl. 1893-1912 (gaps), T. 1895-6, 1912-30; with
abstracts 1869-1916; foster parents' undertakings
1911-17; MO's exam. of children 1915-28.
B. Min's 1835, 1839-1930; C'tee min's: Boarding-
out (with letters) 1910-22, SAC (with letters) 1877-
1903, House 1919-29; out-letters 1878-1918 (gaps);
master's letters 1924-30; various appl 1902-29;
weekly returns 1914-20, 1928-30; appointment of
overseers 1913-20; ledgers 1857-1923; parochial
ledgers 1856-1927; financial statements 1901-13,
1919-28; treasurer's books 1907-14, 1921-30;
collector's ledgers, statements etc. 1909-21, 1925,
1927-30; treasurer's ac's books 1917-26; sup'an.
cert's 1896-7; vouchers etc. 1910-30; poor rate
returns 1899-1929; master's report books 1915-28,
day book 1914-28 (summary 1918-30), receipts and
exp. 1914-34; petty cash 1917-30; requisition lists
1923-27; contracts 1927-8; tenders 1902-3, 1908-9,
1927-29; porter's books 1917-30 (gaps); visitors'
book 1915-26; dietaries 1922-30; provisions issued
etc. 1917-31; medical extras 1923-27, 1929-31;
tobacco and snuff ac's 1917-34; several other ac's
C20; MO's report book 1913-24; Visiting C'tee

papers (lunatics) 1912-32; nurses' report book 1928-9; repayment claims to County Council (lunatics) 1895-1929; casuals medical reports 1923-29; chaplain's report books 1914-30; relieving officer's receipts and exp. books: T. 1910-13, 1916-25; reports on paupers chargeable to T. 1903; maintenance of non-settled poor 1917-30; reports on boarded-out children 1909; oakum ac's 1885-1921; PLC/LGB orders etc. 1901-27.

Public Record Office, *Kew:*
Corres. etc. 1835-1900 [MH 12/8879-95]; staff reg. 1837-1921 [MH 9/17].

Uppingham [3] (Fineshade, Gretton, Harringworth, Laxton, Rockingham, Wakerley).
See under Rutland.

Wellingborough [11] (partly in Beds.).
A. Collector's receipt and exp. books (part) 1905-19; adm. and discharge books 1896-1933; porter's adm. and discharge book 1929-37; inventory of property of deceased inmates 1914-36; bathing reg. 1927-32; births and deaths reg's 1867-1914; infirmary adm. and discharge books 1913-20, 1926-31; creed reg's 1869-c.1930 (1869-98 alphabetical); relieving officer's receipt and exp. books: North 1906-27, South 1909-26; boarded-out children receipt and exp. books 1912 30; out relief order books 1901-28; appl. and report books: North 1906-22, South 1914-24; outdoor relief lists: North 1900-

28, South 1910-24; with abstracts: North 1880-1917, South 1895-1917; boarded-out maintenance pay list 1911-30; reg. of boarded-out children 1902-09; Fairlawn Children's Home adm. and discharge book 1906-54, conduct book 1914-18; vac. reg's: Earl's Barton 1891-1927, Higham Ferrers 1879-1910, Wellingborough 1883-94, Finedon 1920-28.; reg. of infants (life protection) 1904-09; rate book 1854; objections to valuations 1928.
B. Min's 1835-6, 1865-1930 (gaps); C'tee min's: Cottage Homes and Boarding-out 1909-30, Management 1898-1920, House 1917-30, Assessment 1876-81, 1911-21; out-letters 1903-26; weekly returns 1913-30; reg. of overseers 1919-20; call book 1917-22; ledgers 1875-1926; parochial ledgers 1875-84, 1888-1919; financial statements 1905-30; treasurer's book 1911-30; collector's ledgers (South) 1912-24; treasurer's ac's book 1925-27; salaries 1927-29; registrar's return of fees 1911-29; master's report book and journal 1895-1912, day book 1915-19, 1922-28; petty cash 1920-22; wages books 1910-30; provisions receipts etc. 1913-21.

Public Record Office, *Kew:*
Corres. etc. 1835-1900 (missing 1881-82) [MH 12/8898-919]; staff reg. 1837-1921 [MH 9/18].

Unidentified PLU.
The N.R.O. holds various documents, incl. a punishment book 1910-27, and reg. of non-resident poor, whose Union of origin cannot be identified.

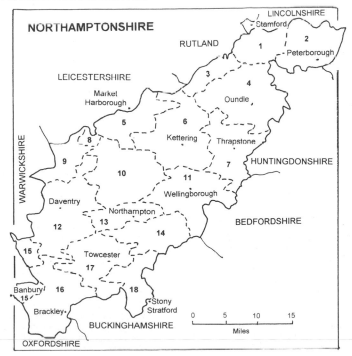

NORTHAMPTONSHIRE

LINCOLNSHIRE
Stamford
RUTLAND
1
2
Peterborough
LEICESTERSHIRE
3
Market Harborough
4
Oundle
5
6
Kettering
Thrapstone
8
HUNTINGDONSHIRE
9
7
10
11
Wellingborough
Daventry
Northampton
12
13
BEDFORDSHIRE
14
15
Towcester
17
Banbury
16
18
15
Stony Stratford
Brackley
BUCKINGHAMSHIRE
OXFORDSHIRE
WARWICKSHIRE

0   5   10   15
Miles

NORTHUMBERLAND

Unless shown otherwise, PLU records are held at **Morpeth Records Centre**, where they can be seen on Wednesdays only. By prior arrangement they can be seen on other working days at **Northumberland Record Office**, Melton Park, North Gosforth, Newcastle upon Tyne, where all enquiries should be addressed.

Records closed or with restricted access are asterisked.

Alnwick [6].
A. *Bastardy order reg. 1852-1916; relieving officer's receipt and exp. book c.1930.
B. Min's 1917-30; C'tee mins; W'h. 1914-30, Assessment 1926-27; ledgers 1920-30; treasurer's ac's 1916-30; securities reg. 1880-1920.
Public Record Office, Kew:
Corres. etc. 1835-1900 [MH 12/8927-49]; staff reg. 1837-1921 [MH 9/1].

Belford [3].
Berwick-upon-Tweed Record Office:
A. Births reg. 1915-32.
B. Min's 1836-1925; C'tee min's: Finance 1896-1913, W'h. 1914-26; ledgers 1929-30; garden and pig ac's 1905-40; *staff service reg. 1897-1930; *officers' appointment reg. c.1877-1929; contracts for post of vac. officer to Belford PLU 1909-23.
Public Record Office, Kew:
Corres. etc. 1835-1904 [MH 12/8954-63]; staff reg. 1837-1904 [MH 9/2].

Bellingham [4].
B. Min's 1881-1913; Assessment C'tee min's 1880-1927; letter books 1876-1905; ledgers 1892-1930; service reg's 1896-1927; vac. officer's report book, n.d.
Public Record Office, Kew:
Corres. etc. 1836-1900 [MH 12/8964-75]; staff reg. 1837-1921 [MH 9/2].

Berwick-on-Tweed [1] (partly in Co. Durham, 1836-44).
Berwick-upon-Tweed Record Office:
A. Rate books: Tweedmouth 1849, 1863, 1881, Longridge 1879-88, Berwick 1885, 1887-88, Ancroft 1919-20; valuation lists 1869-88 (gaps); births and deaths reg's 1837-1914; collector's receipt and exp. books, Kyloe 1848-62; *pauper (children) service book 1853-1925; Children's Home adm. order book 1912-21; *Children's Home relief list 1920-21.
B. Min's 1840-1919; letter books 1852-89; ledgers 1837-1930; parochial ledgers 1848-1927; vagrant provision ac's 1862-69; *service reg. 1896-1922; *superannuation reg's 1896-1929; *contract book 1929-31; establishment and clothing ac's 1844-47.
Public Record Office, Kew:
Corres. etc. 1835-1900 [MH 12/8976-99]; staff reg. 1837-1921 [MH 9/2].

Castle Ward [10].
B. Ledger 1927-30; mortgages reg. 1977-1915.

Public Record Office, Kew:
Corres. etc. 1836-1900 [MH 12/9002-17]; staff reg. 1837-1921 [MH 9/4].

Glendale [2].
Berwick-upon-Tweed Record Office:
B. Min's 1853-87; letter book 1897; *service reg. 1897-1930.
Public Record Office, Kew:
Corres. etc. 1835-1900 [MH 12/9020-31]; staff reg. 1837-1921 [MH 9/7].

Haltwhistle [8].
B. Min's 1900-30; ledgers 1836-1929; treasurer's ac's 1923; parochial ledgers 1900-27; *sup'an. ledger 1896-1929.
Public Record Office, Kew:
Corres. etc. 1835-1900 (missing 1846-53, 1867-Aug. 1871) [MH 12/9032-39]; staff reg. 1837-1921 [MH 9/8].

Hexham [9].
A. Abstract of appl. and report book 1836-38.
B. Min's 1836-1930; C'tee min's: Finance 1895-1928, House 1902-26; House C'tee report books 1921-24; letter books (out) 1881-1927; letter book (removal) 1883-1900; ledgers 1836-1930; treasurer's ac's 1898-1927; parochial ac's 1847-1910; securities reg. 1883; mortgages reg. 1880-1915; financial statements 1916-20; monthly salaries reg. 1925-27; *service reg. 1928 29.
Public Record Office, Kew:
Corres. etc. 1835-1900 [MH 12/9040-66]; staff reg. 1837-1921 [MH 9/8].

Morpeth [7] (partly Co. Durham, 1836-44).
B. Min's 1902-05; ledger 1923-30.
Public Record Office, Kew:
Corres. etc. 1835-1900 [MH 12/9071-91]; staff reg. 1837-1921 [MH 9/11].

Newcastle-on-Tyne [12].
Tyne and Wear Archives Service, Newcastle upon Tyne (abbreviated list):
A. Punishment book 1893-1913; births reg. 1840-1923; relief papers (incl. indoor and outdoor lists) 1848-1930; settlement and removal (incl. reg. of children) c.1886-99; reg. of lunatics 1865-1909; appr. indentures 1808-1927; reg. of pauper servants 1851-c.1930; papers re. emigration of children to Australia, Canada, South Africa etc. 1922-29; vac. reg's 1910-21; reg. of infants received for reward 1902-36.
Newcastle upon Tyne Central Library:
B. Statement of receipts and exp. (ptd.) 1879-89.
University of Durham:
A. Printed Reports of the state of the lying-in Hospital for poor married women in Newcastle 1760-86, with abstract of ac's, account of women adm. and discharged, list of officers and annual subscribers.
Public Record Office, Kew:
Corres. etc. 1835-1900 (missing 1846-50) [MH 12/9096-135]; staff reg. 1837-1921 [MH 9/12].

Rothbury [5].
B. Ledger 1927-30; sup'an ledger 1900-02; corres., papers and ac's 1917-29.
Public Record Office, Kew:
Corres. etc. 1835-1900 [MH 12/9144-54]; staff reg. 1837-1921 [MH 9/14].

Tynemouth [11].
Tyne and Wear Archives Service, Newcastle upon Tyne:
A. Adm. and discharge reg's 1867-1947; creed reg's 1884-1949; reg. of lunatics 1911-48; births reg. 1914-48; deaths reg. 1896-1949; maternity reg. 1910-49; vac. reg's: w'h 1919-45, North Longbenton 1877-92.
B. Min's 1836-1931.
Public Record Office, Kew:
Corres. etc. 1834-1900 [MH 12/9156-207]; staff reg. 1837-1921 [MH 9/17].

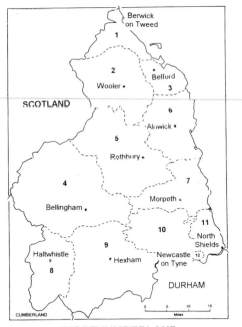

NORTHUMBERLAND

NOTTINGHAMSHIRE

See Notts. Archives Information Sheet *Poor Law Union Records* for a description of the records and summary of classess likely to be of most interest; and M. Caplan, *In the shadow of the workhouse: the implementation of the New Poor Law throughout Nottinghamshire, 1836-1846* (1984).

Unless shown otherwise, records are at ***Nottinghamshire Archives Office, Nottingham***.
N.A.O. also has a large number of papers relating to the assisted emigration scheme to the Cape of Good Hope in 1819-20, and an index of those in receipt of such assistance covering 111 documents. See 'Notts. settlers in the Cape of Good Hope', *A Notts. Miscellany*, Thoroton Soc. Record Series **21** (1962).

Basford [8] (partly Derbys.).
See T. Fry, 'A look at the Basford Union Workhouse', *Notts. F.H.S.* **5**.11 (1988); and C.P. Griffin, 'Chartism and opposition to the New Poor Law in Nottinghamshire: the Basford Union workhouse affair of 1844', *Midland History* **2** (1973/4).
A. Adm. and discharge books 1854-57; outdoor relief lists 1900-30; DMOs' relief books 1857-65, 1915-6, 1922, 1928; vac. reg's (various districts) 1887-1916 (gaps); appr's indentures and settlement (179) 1845-1903 (names in catalogue, indexed); reg. of children in w'h. c.1900-30, and list 1915; reg. of boarded-out orphans 1928-30, valuation lists 1910: Annesley, Awsworth, Bestwood Park (also 1904, 1924), Brinsley, Burton Joyce (1897, 1900 only), Cossall, Gedling, Greasley, Kimberley, Lambley, Linby (also 1904), Newstead (also 1904, 1924), Nuttall, Papplewick, Ruddington, Selston, Trowell, Woodborough (1904 only).
B. Min's 1836-1930; C'tee min's: Boarding-out 1920-30, Finance 1909-30, House 1915-30, Visiting 1906-15, Vac. 1907-29, Children 1909-15, Special (Office) 1909-29, SAC 1877-1903; year books 1917-26 (gaps); PLC orders 1838-1917; estimates of receipts and exp. (half yearly) 1891-1924; statements 1920-30; plans etc. 1900, 1911-17; tenders and contracts 1913-30; staff insurance policies 1894-1926; orphans receipt and exp. ac's 1911-30; letter books 1845-1929; treasurer's ac's 1919-30; monthly salaries ac's 1912-30; dietary 1920; collector's statement of rates 1911; school fees order book 1889-91.
County Local Studies Library, Nottingham:
Printed lists: paupers 1897-8; Guardians 1866-1891, 1926.
Public Record Office, Kew:
Corres. etc. 1835-1900 [MH 12/9228-93]; staff reg. 1837-1921 [MH 9/2].

Bingham [12] (partly Leics.)
A. Births reg. 1837-1930; vac. reg's, Radcliffe 1866-1921 (incl. Bingham from 1879); valuation lists 1897-1929 (occasional years only); collector's ac's of contributions 1899-1911 (indexed), receipts and exp. 1897-1922.

B. Min's 1836-1930; C'tee min's: Finance 1879-1916, Assessment 1862-1925; year books 1907-8, 1913-4; parochial ledger 1907-29; treasurer's ac's 1923-30; receipts and exp. 1921-30; vac. officer's report book 1898-1904.
Public Record Office, Kew:
Corres. etc. 1835-1900 [MH 12/9315-32]; staff reg. 1837-1921 [MH 9/2].

Doncaster [1] (Auckley, Finningley, Misson).
See under Yorkshire West Riding.

East Retford see **Retford, East**.

Gainsborough [4] (Beckingham, Bole, West Burton, Misterton, Saundby, West Stockwith, Walkeringham).
See under Lincolnshire (Pts. Lindsey).

Loughborough [13] (Costock, East and West Leake, Normanton on Soar, Rempstone, Stanford on Soar, Sutton Bonington, Thorpe in the Glebe, Willoughby on the Wolds, Wysall).
See under Nottinghamshire.

Mansfield [5] (partly Derbys.).
A. Relief order book 1929-30; relief lists and clerk's cash ac's for boarded-out children 1924-29; creed reg. (Cottage Home) 1913-35; vac. reg's 1923-30; rate books: Mansfield Woodhouse 1891, Sookholme 1914, 1916; collector's receipts and exp. 1926.
B. Min's 1838-1930; C'tee min's: Building 1909-30, Cottage Homes 1906-21, Finance 1911-30, House 1909-30, Infirmary 1910-14; annual list of Guardians and paid officers 1839-1921, and other staff 1874-1919; salaries journals 1910-30; ledgers 1924-30; treasurer's ac's 1924-30; receipts and exp. 1929-30; parochial ledger 1923-28; receipts and exp. book 1907-29; w'h. plans 1908, 1914, 1920s; ag'mts (various) and schedule of deeds 1896-1930; reg. of securities 1867-1905; overseers' ac's: Mansfield 1869-1917, Mansfield Woodhouse 1877-1923; master's receipts and exp. 1905-07; wages ac's 1907-30; inventories 1930; abstracts of outdoor relief 1898-1920; collector's ledger 1908-19; Assessment C'tee min's 1897-1910, 1924-27.
Public Record Office, Kew:
Corres. etc. 1835-1900 [MH 12/9356-98]; staff reg. 1837-1921 [MH 9/11].

Melton Mowbray (Upper Broughton).
See under Leicestershire.

Newark [7] (partly Leics.).
A. Reg. of non-resident poor 1909-13; vac. reg's (various) 1881-1932; list of children boarded-out 1919; claims for maintenance of (named) lunatics 1896-1916.
B. Min's 1836-1930; C'tee min's: Assessment 1881-1904, Boarding-out 1908-23, Cottage Home 1913-30, House 1909-30, Infirmary and Vagrant Wards 1904-09, Settlement 1905-6, Printing and stationery 1905-15; Guardians' attendance reg. 1915-30; declarations of office 1895-1928; year

books 1905-16; treasurer's ac's 1905-30; financial statements 1910-27, 1930; out-county salary claims 1901-22; weekly returns 1922-30; w'h. plans c.1915-30; contracts etc. 1920-30; reg. of securities 1877-1907; mortgages 1875-77; LGB orders 1905, 1907; Boarding-out C'tee visitors' weekly exp. book 1920-23; out letters 1914-31; treasurer's receipts and exp. 1903-08, 1912-30; master's wages receipt books 1912-20, 1922-29; reg. of salaries and sup'an. 1901-c.1911; inventories 1930.
Lincolnshire Archives Office, Lincoln:
A. Out relief ac's for vagrants and bastardy 1834-39; valuation lists (various) between 1888 and 1919.
B. Tenders 1816-68; ledger (Claypole House of Industry) 1818-48.
Public Record Office, Kew:
Corres. etc. 1835-1900 [MH 12/9411-38]; staff reg. 1837-1921 [MH 9/12].

Nottingham [9].
See Notts. Archives Information Sheet *Nottingham Union Workhouse Registers* for a description of the contents of various reg's listed below.
A. Corres. etc. relating to individual cases of settlement (712) 1901-07 (listed alphabetically in catalogue); adm. and discharge reg's 1856-1920 (casuals 1892-1939); deaths reg's 1851-2, 1861-2, 1864-85, 1890-1926 (infirmary 1908-20); indoor relief lists 1858-1910 (indexed from 1863); medical relief (w'h.) 1899; creed reg's 1881-1942 (gaps).
B. Min's 1893-95 (only); printed min's 1908, 1926; unofficial notebook of Richard Sutton, member of Board 1837-8; reports and abstracts of ac's 1893, 1901-09, 1915-29; C'tee min's (various) 1916-29; letter book 1836-41; LGB corres. 1883-1902; out-letter books 1914-30; ledgers 1838-40, 1908-10; overseers' ac's 1917-27; draft ac's 1905-6, 1912-3; visitors' book 1914; master's report books 1903-32; receipts and exp. 1885-1905; wages and salaries books 1913-44 (various categories, weeded, so only occasional periods); Assessment C'tee min's 1885-88 (indexed), out-letters 1914-16, 1919-21.
County Local Studies Library, Nottingham:
B. Printed abstracts of ac's (listing staff) 1893-1922.
Public Record Office, Kew:
Corres. etc. 1835-1900 [MH 12/9444-99]; staff reg. 1837-1921 [MH 9/12].

Radford [10] (1836-97; merged with Nottingham).
A. Indoor relief list 1879-80 (amongst Nottingham PLU records).
No other locally held records known.
Public Record Office, Kew:
Corres. etc. 1835-1882 [MH 12/9511-23]; staff reg. 1837-1897 [MH 9/14].

Retford, East [3].
A. Vac. reg's 1871-1919.
B. Min's 1836-1930; C'tee min's: House 1914-30, Boarding-out 1912-28, Relief recovery 1920-26, Assessment 1910-27; ledgers 1913-30; treasurer's ledgers 1916-23; parochial ledgers 1910-27;

financial statements 1918-30; petty cash book 1901-27; reg. of mortgages 1900-28; boarding-out receipt and exp. book 1923-30; boarded-out children maintenance pay list 1924-30; treasurer's receipt and exp. book 1926-30; loan ac's 1928-30; w'h. day book 1838-43.

Public Record Office, *Kew:*
Corres. etc. 1835-1900 [MH 12/9333-53]; staff reg. 1837-1921 [MH 9/6].

Shardlow [11] (Bramcote, Chilwell, Kingston on Soar, Ratcliffe on Soar, Stapleford, Toton).
See under Derbyshire.

Southwell [6].

A. Maintenance pay list of boarded-out children 1922-30; reg. of lunatics 1891-1928; bathing reg's 1914-31; punishment book 1852-1936; outdoor relief lists 1923-4, 1927-8; collector's receipts and exp. (Clipstone) 1927-29; vac. reg's 1871-79, 1910-21; list of unvac. children 1914-20.

B. Min's 1836-1930, C'tee min's: Boarding-out 1910-30, House 1909-14, 1921-30, SAC 1877-1903, Assessment 1862-1927; ledgers: 1836-1905 (gaps) (incl. parochial ac's to 1847), 1914-16, 1924-27, parochial 1848-65, 1912-27, non-settled poor 1866-1910, 1923-30; treasurer's ac's 1916-20, 1923-30, financial statements 1921-30; weekly returns 1927-30; w'h. plans c.1930; req. of securities 1915-30; boarding-out receipts and exp. (summaries) 1920 30; reg. of wool sales 1875-83; PL officers' journal 1917 (part indexed); treasurer's receipts and exp. ac's 1911-17, 1923-30; relieving officer's recipts and exp. (North District) 1907-10, 1922-24, 1926-28; vac. officer's summaries 1907-23 and report books 1908-20, vac. report books 1908-20; return of deaths under 12 months 1902.

Public Record Office, *Kew:*
Corres. etc. 1835-1900 [MH 12/9524-46]; staff reg 1837-1921 [MH 9/15].

Thurgarton Hundred (Union incorporated 1824).
A. List of w'h. inmates 1833-36.
B. Ag'mt to build w'h. 1824-5; ac's 1824-46; inventories 1833-36.

Worksop [2] (partly Derbys., Yorks. W.R.).
A. Non-settled poor ac's 1930; relief order books: North dist. 1926-7, South dist. 1924-29, Worksop 1925-6; reg. of appr's 1879-89, 1909; reg. of children boarded-out 1911-29; Children's Homes reg. 1901-30; collector's receipts and exp. 1922-27; vac. reg's: Worksop 1910-21, Carlton 1902-21, Whitwell and Elmton 1921-26, Clown 1923-27; Valuation lists: various places between 1863 and 1886, Harworth 1911, Worksop ?1913.

B. Min's 1848-1930 (gaps); C'tee min's (various) 1901-04, 1911-30, Assessment 1862-77, 1888-1927; Guardians' declarations 1895-1928; parochial ledger ac's 1874-78, 1927-30; petty cash ac's 1917-34; financial statements 1927, 1930; weekly returns (stat's) 1921-27; w'h. plan c.1930; reg. of securities

(mortgages) 1884-1928; Boarding-out C'tee ac's 1911-30; treasurer's receipts and exp. 1921-30, loan ac's 1899-1930; wages receipt books (Infirmary) 1911-30; Children's Homes: superintendent's day books 1915-25, provision and necessaries ac's 1917-26; relieving officers' weekly summaries 1923-27 and ac's (Worksop district) 1923-29; collector's ledgers 1921, 1925-28; vac. officers' summaries 1907-24 and reports 1907-27; returns of deaths under 12 months 1915; other returns 1911-25.

Worksop Library:
B. Finance C'tee ac's (printed) 1928-9.

Public Record Office, *Kew:*
Corres. etc. 1835-1900 [MH 12/9549-71]; staff reg. 1837-1921 [MH 9/19].

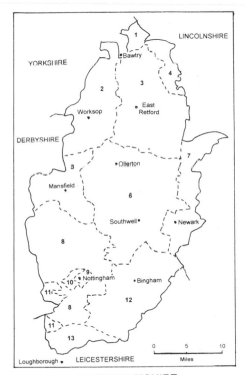

NOTTINGHAMSHIRE

RUTLAND

Oakham [1] (partly in Leics.).
Leicestershire Record Office, Wigston Magna.
B. Min's 1836-1930.
Public Record Office, Kew:
Corres. etc. 1834-1900 [MH 12/9753-805]; staff reg. 1837-1921 [MH 9/12].

Stamford [2] (Gt. and Lit. Casterton, Clipsham, Essendine, Ketton, Pickworth, Ryhall, Tinwell, Tixover).
See under Lincolnshire (Pts. Kesteven).

Uppingham [3] (partly in Leics. and Northants.).
Leicestershire Record Office, Wigston Magna.
B. Min's 1836-1930; ledgers 1894-1949; letter books 1913-21; service reg's 1897-1930.
Public Record Office, Kew:
Corres. etc. 1834-1900 [MH 12/9806-21]; staff reg. 1837-1921 [MH 9/17].

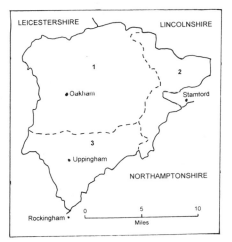

RUTLAND

STAFFORDSHIRE

Most records are at *Staffordshire Record Office, Stafford*. Details of holdings are based on the summary list at the front of the catalogue, so do not necessarily shows minor gaps in chronological coverage or all classes of surviving records. There is a 50 year closure period for PL records.

Alstonfield (Gilbert Union to 1869, then see Ashbourne and Leek).

Ashbourne [26] (Alstonfield (from 1869), Blore with Swinscoe, Calton, Calwich, Ellastone, Ilam, Mayfield, Okeover, Prestwood, Ramshorn, Stanton, Waterfall, Wetton (from 1869), Woodhouses, Wootton).
See under Derbyshire.

Bromsgrove [22] (Clent).
See under Worcestershire.

Bromwich, West see under **West Bromwich.**

Burton upon Trent [11] (partly Derbys.).
Burton upon Trent Library:
A. Births and deaths reg's 1837-1879; adm's and discharges c.1880-1930.
B. Min's 1837-1930; relieving officers' weekly reports (Southern Dist.) 1843-45.
Public Record Office, Kew:
Corres. etc. 1834-1900 (missing 1839-42) [MH 12/11232-66]; staff reg. 1837-1921 [MH 9/3].

Cannock [13] (formerly Penkridge).
Staffordshire Record Office, Stafford:
A. Outdoor relief lists 1836, 1839.
B. Min's 1836-45; ledgers 1927-30; overseers' balance sheets 1898-1921.
Public Record Office, Kew:
Corres. etc. 1848-1900 (missing Aug. 1871-73, 1887-88) [MH 12/11389-410]; staff reg. 1836-75 (Penkridge) [MH 9/13], 1872 on (Cannock) [MH 9/4].

Cheadle [5].
See published history, 1735-1987 (pamphlet).
Staffordshire Record Office, Stafford:
B. Min's 1837-1930; Children's Home C'tee 1916-30; ledgers 1864-1930; parochial ledgers 1907-27; treasurer's ac's 1914-29; staff salaries 1914; DMO's relief books, Ipstones, 1919-26; receipts and exp. 1837-89; statement of ac's 1843-45.
Public Record Office, Kew:
Corres. etc. 1834-1900 [MH 12/11276-95]; staff reg. 1837-1921 [MH 9/4].

Congleton [2] (Biddulph).
See under Cheshire.

Dudley [19] (partly Worcs.)
Dudley Archives and Local History Service, Coseley:
A. Adm. and discharge reg's 1839-41, 1850-58, 1862-67, 1871-75, 1879-83, 1892-94, 1912-24, 1926-29; porter's adm. and discharge reg's 1898-9, 1915-17, 1924; lists of persons in receipt of relief ✒

Staffordshire: Dudley *continued*

(printed?) 1908, 1910; indoor relief list and abstract 1911; creed reg's 1868-1900, 1913-23, 1926-33; reg. of pauper lunatics 1904-14; reg's of removal orders 1903-30; return of births registered and vac. reg. (Sedgley dist.) 1921-23.

B. Min's 1836-1923; C'tee min's: various between 1888 and 1930, Assessment 1863-1913, Boarding-out 1910-17, 1925-30, Building 1904-20, Children's Homes (incl. sub-c'tees) 1905-30, Contracts 1906-24, Farm 1901-29, Finance 1885-88, 1897-1900, 1902-11, 1913-25, Removal, Enquiry and Payment of Relief 1901-30 (with repayment case books 1906-30), Visiting 1859-70, 1904-25; Dudley ratepayers re. poll 1853-56; letter books 1858-1902; returns: receipts and exp. and loan ac's 1890-1902, 1907-24, weekly numbers of paupers 1912-29 (missing 1926), appointment of staff 1882-96; reg. of contracts 1908-14; misc. printed reports 1902-05; printed ac's 1903-25; forms re. repayment by C.C. for maintenance of lunatics 1917-20; lists of contractors 1922-30; petty cash book 1923-30; declarations of acceptance of office as Guardians 1928; ledgers 1837-1927; treasurer's ledgers 1909-27; parochial ledgers 1848-1901, 1912-3; sup'an. service reg. 1896-1902; salaries ledgers 1907-13; half-yearly summaries of ac's 1902-15, 1926-28; plans 1883.

Staffordshire Record Office, Stafford:
A. Receipts and exp.: Coseley 1924-27, Rowley Regis 1923-24; vac. reg's (Dudley, Rowley Regis, Sedgley, Tipton) 1915-35.
B. Ledgers 1922-30; master's receipts and exp. 1919-21; wages book 1929-30; master's daybook 1924-27; provisions ac's book 1922-24 etc.; collectors' ledgers (Sedgley, Coseley, Rowley Regis) 1925-31.

Public Record Office, Kew:
Corres. etc. 1834-1900 [MH 12/13958-93 (under Worcs.)]; staff reg. 1837-1921 [MH 9/6]

Kidderminster [21] (Upper Arley, Broom).
See under Worcestershire.

King's Norton [24] (Harborne, Smethwick).
See under Worcestershire.

Leek [1].
Staffordshire Record Office, Stafford:
A. Relieving officer's appl. and report book 1845-46.
B. Min's 1837-1930; Finance C'tee min's 1886-94; ledgers 1838-1928; parochial ledgers 1848-1912; treasurer's ac's 1838-1929; non-settled poor ledger 1845-56; building loan ac's book 1838-52; treasurer's receipts and exp. 1866-67; House C'tee reports 1916-29.
Public Record Office, Kew:
Corres. etc. 1834-1900 (missing Aug. 1887 - May 1891) [MH 12/11297-323]; staff reg. 1837-1921 [MH 9/10].

Lichfield [14].
Staffordshire Record Office, Stafford:
. **A.** Inmates 1924-28; valuation lists 1868-1934; rate books 1866-1957.
B. Min's 1836-1930; C'tee min's: W'h. 1909-12, Relief 1921-30, Non-settled poor 1913-30, Children's 1913-30, Finance 1884-1930; inventories 1915-37; ledgers 1883-1930; treasurer's ac's 1915-30; parochial ledgers 1886-1927; reg. of securities 1873-1908; petty cash ledgers 1918-30.
Public Record Office, Kew:
Corres. etc. 1834-1900 [MH 12/11330-58]; staff reg. 1837-1921 [MH 9/10].

Market Drayton [6] (Ashley, Mucklestone, Tyrley).
See under Shropshire.

Newcastle under Lyme [25].
Staffordshire Record Office, Stafford:
A. Relieving officers' appl. and report books 1902-21; medical relief lists 1904-15; SAC records 1878-79; vac. reg's 1881-1920.
B. Min's 1837-1930; House C'tee min's 1914-30; ledgers 1843-1930; treasurer's ac's 1922-29; parochial ledgers 1902-26; returns of births and deaths 1894-1924.
Public Record Office, Kew:
Corres. etc. 1834-1900 [MH 12/11363-83]; staff reg. 1837-1921 [MH 9/12].

Newport [8] (Adbaston, Forton, Gnosall, Norbury, High Offley, Weston Jones)
See under Shropshire.

Penkridge see **Cannock**.

Seisdon [16] (partly Shrops.).
Staffordshire Record Office, Stafford:
A. W'h. adm. and discharge books 1837-1916, indoor relief lists 1837-1930; creed reg. 1869-91; reg. of infants received c.1912-29; births reg. 1853-1914; list of paupers and statement of ac's, Trysull, 1852-58; removal order file 1856.
B. Min's 1852-1930; ledgers 1848-1930; parochial ledgers 1852-1920; financial statements 1890-95.
Wolverhampton Central Library (Archives):
B. Assessment C'tee min's 1901-27.
Public Record Office, Kew:
Corres. etc. 1844-1900 (missing 1889-92) [MH 12/11413-25]; staff reg. 1837-1921 [MH 9/15].

Shifnal [12] (Blymhill, Patshull, Sheriff Hales, Weston under Lizard).
See under Shropshire.

Stafford [9].
Staffordshire Record Office, Stafford:
A. Out-relief order books 1913-17; appr. reg's 1885-99; removal orders 1886-88; w'h. adm. and discharge reg's 1842-1930 (vagrants 1916-30); births reg. 1914-30; cert's of baptisms in the w'h. 1900-27; deaths reg. 1858-1930; removal orders 1842-45; indoor relief lists 1839-1918; relieving officer's appl. and report books 1912-18; poor rate books 1897-1926; valuation lists 1848-1922.

Staffordshire: Stafford *continued*

B. Min's 1836-1925; agendas 1904-19; C'tee min's: Finance 1914-29, House 1906-76, Children's Home 1926-30; ledgers 1836-1930; parochial ledgers 1847-1910; estimates of income and exp. 1892-96; financial statements 1900-12; overseers' balance sheets 1878-1927, ac's 1895-1915; collectors' records 1898-1927, monthly statements 1921-27; corres. 1891-1903; treasurer's books 1869-1911; master's reports 1914-29, ac's 1914-30; Visiting C'tee report book 1889-1925.
Public Record Office, Kew:
Corres. etc. 1834-1900 [MH 12/11428-55]; staff reg. 1837-1921 [MH 9/16].

Stoke on Trent [4] (and Wolstanton from 1922).
Stoke City Central Library, Hanley:
B. Min's 1876-1922 (partially printed from 1892); year books 1915-21; diary 1921-2; as Stoke and Wolstanton PLU: min's (printed) 1910-1 (sic), 1922-23, 1925-8, 1930; year books and diaries 1922-30.
Staffordshire Record Office, Stafford:
B. Bills, ac's re. building of Spittals w'h. 1842-45; corres. 1870-99.
Public Record Office, Kew:
Corres. etc. 1834-1900 (missing 1850-54) [MH 12/11458-98]; staff reg. 1837-1921 [MH 9/16].

Stone [7].
Staffordshire Record Office, Stafford:
A. Vac. reg's 1872-85; removal orders and exam's, Sandon, 1834-43; poor rate book, Sandon, 1856.
B. Min's 1837-1930; Finance 1914-30; ledgers 1838-1925; treasurer's ac's 1913-30; parochial ledgers 1855-1928; non-resident and non-settled poor ledgers 1845-47; treasurer's receipts and exp. 1916-28; master's reports 1920-22, day book 1929-30; Assessment C'tee min's 1894-1927; min's of evidence re. master and w'h. 1874; collecting and deposit book 1922-23.
Public Record Office, Kew:
Corres. etc. 1836-1900 [MH 12/11509-28]; staff reg. 1837-1921 [MH 9/16].

Stourbridge [23] (Amblecote, Brierley Hill, Kingswinford, Quarry Bank).
See under Worcestershire.

Tamworth [15] (partly Warw., Derbys.).
Staffordshire Record Office, Stafford:
A. Creed reg. 1912-23; births reg. 1837-1935; deaths reg. 1836-1949; infants deaths 1927-29; punishments 1868-1914; indoor relief lists 1836-1930; adm. and discharge books 1836-1930 (children 1915-30); appl. and report books 1838-1920; valuation lists, Thorpe Constantine, 1876-89; rate books C19.
B. Min's 1836-1930; General Purposes C'tee min's 1910-30; other c'tee min's c.1900-30; ledgers 1836-1930; treasurer's receipts and exp. 1900-07; parochial ledgers 1850-1930; master's reports and journals 1915-32, receipts and exp. 1908-14; visiting c'tee reports 1905-28; overseers' ac's 1849-1908;

statements of ac's 1891-99; MO's reports etc. 1912-24; Children's Home min's etc. 1907-30.
Public Record Office, Kew:
Corres. etc. 1834-1900 (missing 1884, 1891) [MH 12/11532-55]; staff reg. 1837-1921 [MH 9/17].

Uttoxeter [10] (partly Derbys.).
Staffordshire Record Office, Stafford:
B. Min's 1847-1930; ledgers 1897-1930; parochial ledgers 1879-1918; Assessment C'tee 1863-1949; tenders 1928; contract for building w'h. 1838; corres. 1903-17.
Public Record Office, Kew:
Corres. etc. 1834-1900 [MH 12/11559-75]; staff reg. 1837-1921 [MH 9/17].

Walsall [18].
Walsall Local History Centre:
'Most of the records have not been traced and are believed to have been destroyed.'
A. Reg. of lunatics 1877-1928.
B. Min's 1836-39 (indexed, damaged), 1928-30; C'tee min's: General Purposes 1926-30 (sub-c'tees 1911-26), Finance 1926-30, House 1924-30, Boarding-out 1927-30; PLC orders 1836-57; advertisements book 1895-1930; newscuttings 1924-44; MoH circulars 1924-30.
Staffordshire Record Office, Stafford:
A. Poor rate ac's book, Aldridge, 1914, 1917.
Public Record Office, Kew:
Corres. etc. 1834-1900 [MH 12/11578-617]; staff reg. 1837-1921 [MH 9/17].

West Bromwich [20] (partly Shrops., Worcs.).
Staffordshire Record Office, Stafford:
A. Vac. reg's 1920-35.
Sandwell M.B. Local Studies Library, Oldbury, Warley:
B. Min's 1891-1912; Assessment C'tee min's 1862, 1881, 1888, 1897, 1906.
Public Record Office, Kew:
Corres. etc. 1834-1900 [MH 12/11625-63]; staff reg. 1837-1921 [MH 9/18].

Wolstanton and Burslem [3] (amalgamated with Stoke 1922).
Staffordshire Record Office, Stafford:
B. Min's 1838-1914; W'h. Visiting c'tee 1869-1907; letter books 1862-1911; print of new w'h. at Chell, n.d.
Stoke City Central Library, Hanley:
A. Westcliff Institution, Chell: list of reg's of births, baptisms, deaths and of inmates, showing religious creed, alphabetical, various years, mainly 1840's to 1940's.
B. Min's: 1854-58, 1901-03, 1914-16, 1919-22.
Public Record Office, Kew:
Corres. etc. 1835-1900 [MH 12/11196-225]; staff reg. 1837-1921 [MH 9/19].

Wolverhampton [17].
See David E. Wood, 'Poor Law in Wolverhampton 1870-1900' (1986 unpublished Wolverhampton Polytechnic BA dissertation).

Wolverhampton Central Library (Archives):

A. Inmates of children's cottage homes, 1890-1930 (restricted for 100 years).

B. Min's 1839-1915, (printed:) 1913, 1916, 1920-30; C'tee min's: Assessment 1862-1909, Finance 1899-1930, General Purposes 1899-1919, House 1900-23, (combined) 1923-30, G.P. sub-c'tee, W'h. Accommodation, Wolverhampton Wards, Finance and Infant Life Protection 1895-99, W'h. Visiting 1892-1900, Cottage Homes 1890-1930, Farm 1899-1922, School 1885-90, Infirmary 1918-24, Boarding-out and Children Act 1910-30, Dispensary 1899-1930, Misc. 1900-17, Probationary Nurses 1924-30, Repayment of relief 1900-30 (1915-30 closed to public), New W'h. 1898-1903, W'h. Accommodation and Relief Districts 1886-88; cash book 1877-84; master's reports and journal 1842-45; reg. of securities 1869-1927; overseers' min's 1860-1910; Heath Town overseers' min's 1913-27; photos of w'h's, cottage homes, inmates, C19-20; lease of old w'h. 1841; overseers' ac's book 1834-5; out relief ac's 1896-1912; plans of New Cross w'h. 1901-2; records of cottage homes 1890-1977; poor rate returns 1857-1912; Guardians elected 1808-1915; article on Wolverhampton w'h. 1886.

Public Record Office, *Kew:*

Corres. etc. 1834-1900 (missing May 1884 - Apr. 1885) [MH 12/11674-716]; staff reg. 1837-1921 [MH 9/19].

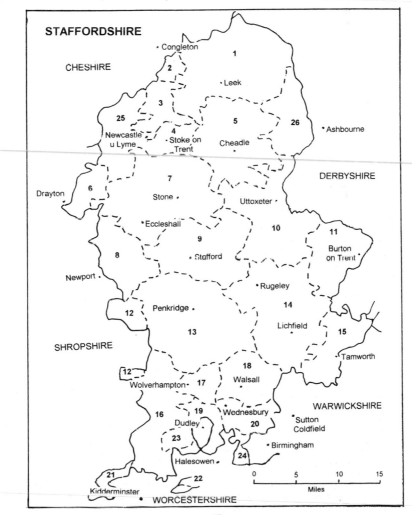

STAFFORDSHIRE

CHESHIRE

• Congleton

1

2

• Leek

3

25

4

• Newcastle u Lyme

• Stoke on Trent

5

Cheadle

26

• Ashbourne

DERBYSHIRE

7

Drayton

6

Stone •

Uttoxeter •

• Eccleshall

10

11

Burton on Trent

9

8

• Stafford

Newport •

• Rugeley

12

Penkridge •

14

13

Lichfield

15

SHROPSHIRE

Tamworth

12

18

Wolverhampton •

17

Walsall

WARWICKSHIRE

16

19

Wednesbury

• Sutton Coldfield

Dudley

20

23

• Birmingham

24

Halesowen •

21

22

0   5   10   15

Kidderminster

Miles

WORCESTERSHIRE

WARWICKSHIRE

The PLU in which each parish lay is shown in June Watkins and Pauline Saul, *Tracing your Ancestors in Warwickshire* (4th edn., B.& M. S.G.H., 1996), based on White's 1851 Directory.

Most records are at
Warwick County Record Office, Warwick.

The following is a brief guide to the records; some records containing more sensitive material, especially relating to children, may be closed for between 50 and 100 years.

Alcester [14] (partly Worcs.)
Warwick County Record Office, Warwick:
A. Adm. and discharges 1902-32; out relief 1837-1847, 1928-39; indoor relief 1838-47; vac. reg's 1887-1908; reg. of lunatics 1877-1930; births reg. 1836-68; reg. of children boarded-out c.1908-28; reg. of friends and relatives 1900-45.
B. Min's 1859-1930; ac's 1836-1929; MO reports 1906-39.
Public Record Office, Kew:
Corres. etc. 1834-1896 [MH 12/13218-30]; staff reg. 1837-1921 [MH 9/1].

Aston [2] (1836-1911, thereafter **Birmingham**).
Birmingham Central Library (Archives):
A. Maintenance of pauper lunatics 1899-1911; reg. of adopted children 1903-11; reg. of deserted children 1897-1912; reg. of servants and appr's 1882-93; deaths of infants (returns to vac. office) 1891, 1903-06; reg. of children boarded-out 1904-1912; relief order book 1908-11; vac. reg's 1886-92, 1906-7. The following Children's Home records are closed for 100 years: reg's of children 1889-1924; baptisms reg. 1900-31; deaths reg. 1902-08.
B. Min's 1836-1912; 'numerous' c'tee and sub-c'tee min's; ledgers 1845-86; financial statements 1900-1912; loan statements 1892-1912; LGB letters 1892-1912, orders 1836-1911.
Public Record Office, Kew:
Corres. etc. 1834-1896 [MH 12/13232-67]; staff reg. 1837-1921 [MH 9/1].

Atherstone [5] (partly Leics.).
Warwick County Record Office, Warwick:
B. Min's 1863-1930; ac's 1855-1930.
Public Record Office, Kew:
Corres. etc. 1834-1896 [MH 12/13270-84]; staff reg. 1837-1921 [MH 9/1].

Banbury [18] (Avon Dassett, Farnborough, Mollington, Radway, Ratley and Upton, Shotteswell, Warmington).
See under Oxfordshire.

Birmingham [20] (Incorporation/PLU from 1783).
See R.J. Hetherington, 'Birmingham W'h Records', *Midland Ancestor*, **9**.8 (June 1991), p. 319.
Birmingham Central Library (Archives):
A. Admissions reg. (later Dudley Road Hospital) c.1890-1960 (see *Warwickshire History*, **9**.5 (Summer 1995); Appl's and report book 1842; vac. reg. (St. Martin's) 1924-28; appr. indentures, mostly

C19; Marston Green Cottage Home reg's (closed for 100 years): adm. and discharges, reg's of children, baptisms reg's c.1880-1934.
B. Min's 1783-1930 (c.1880 missing); C'tee min's: Finance 1847-1930, Central Relief and Dispensary (later, Central Relief) 1877-1939, General Purposes (later General Purposes and Advisory) 1852-1930, and various others; cash books 1799-1847 (gaps); non-settled poor ledgers 1845-61; non-resident poor ledgers 1824-48; outdoor receipt and exp. book 1899-1903; receipts and exp. books 1822-39; ledgers 1841, 1857, 1870-1; financial statements 1890-94; loan ac's book 1896-1912; PLC/PLB/LGB corres. 1870-1912, returns 1879-1911, and orders 1837-1912; appointment of Guardians 1895-1910; surveyor's report book on poor rate appeals 1865-1868.
Public Record Office, Kew:
Corres. etc. 1834-1896 [MH 12/13286-68]; staff reg. 1837-1921 [MH 9/2, MH 9/20].

Bromsgrove [13] (Tardebigge, to 1844).
See under Worcestershire).

Chipping Norton [19] (Barton on the Heath, Little and Long Compton).
See under Oxfordshire.

Coventry [21] (Incorporation/PLU).
See P. Searby, 'The relief of the poor in Coventry 1830-1863', *The Historical Journal* **20** (1977).
Coventry City Record Office:
Coventry had an unusual PL history in C19. Many of the suburbs were placed in other PLUs (**Foleshill, Meriden,** and **Warwick**), while until 1874 the city centre parishes remained under the 1801 Act which had united them. What follows summarises the surviving records between 1801 and 1930.
A. Removal orders 1659-1812 (on microfilm); parochial reg's, various, 1897-1906; ag'mt to place 15 girls at Tutbury 1802; adm. and discharge books 1853-1946 (gaps); reg. of inmates 1901-44 (index 1898-1927); births reg. 1875-1933; deaths reg. 1845-1943; reg. of lunatics in w'h. 1915-26; creed reg's 1861-1943; indoor relief lists 1851-1940 (gaps); reg. of inmates' property 1856-1929; ac's and assessments (St. Michael's) 1732-1830.
B. Min's 1801-1930; C'tee min's: SAC 1877-1903, Boarding-out 1891-1948, Overseers' 1896-1926; ledgers 1919-23; stock receipts 1922; year books 1914-29; boundary case 1898; proposed infirmary 1884; overseers' appointments 1874, 1922; instructions to registrars and enumerators re. 1911 census; vac.: contracts 1878-1920, corres. 1898-1929; MoH: contracts 1878-1920, corres. 1903-1920; dietaries 1901; w'h. rules 1842; LGB orders and letters 1871-1925; reg. of officers' guarantees 1920-30; reg. of annual subscriptions and rents 1890-1931; election papers, various, 1901-07; insurance papers 1892-1832, incl. insured staff; Union boundary ag'mt 1902; treasurer's bond 1907; draft sewage ag'mt 1886; deeds, mortgages, maps etc. 1916;receipt and exp. book and vouchers for children's maintenance 1913-20; maps and plans

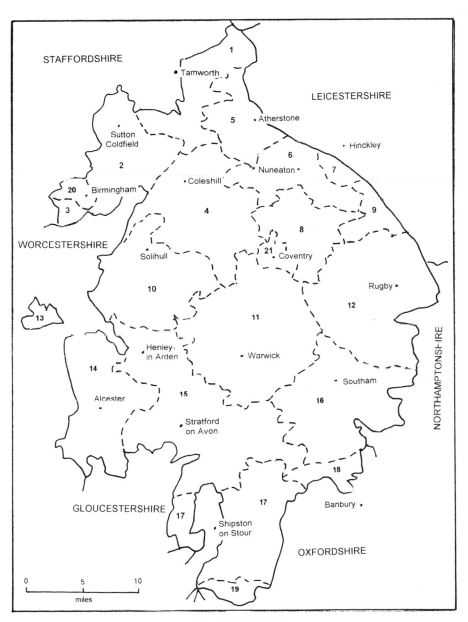

STAFFORDSHIRE

1

• Tamworth

LEICESTERSHIRE

5   • Atherstone

Sutton
Coldfield

• Hinckley

2

6

Nuneaton •

7

20   Birmingham

• Coleshill

3

4

9

WORCESTERSHIRE

8

Solihull •

21 • Coventry

10

Rugby •

13

12

Henley•
in Arden

• Warwick

14

• Southam

Alcester

15

16

•

• Stratford
on Avon

18

GLOUCESTERSHIRE

17

17

Banbury •

Shipston
on Stour

OXFORDSHIRE

NORTHAMPTONSHIRE

0   5   10

miles

19

WARWICKSHIRE

WORCESTERSHIRE

Unless shown otherwise, records are at
*Hereford and Worcester Record Office H.Q.,
Spetchley Road, Worcester*

General papers relating to several or all unions:
A. Exam. and removal cert's C17-19.
B. Deeds 1891-1955; general orders 1836-47;
Union returns on rateable values 1873-89 and
assessments 1874; PLC papers (HM Treasury)
1834-46; Min's of various joint c'tees under 1894
LG Act; mortgages 1902-25; 'Palfrey collection'
scrapbook on Unions etc.; dietaries 1687-1974.

Alcester [12] (Abbots Morton, Feckenham,
Inkberrow, (Upper) Ipsley, Oldborrow).
See under Warwickshire.

Bromsgrove [6] (partly Warws., Shrops., Staffs.).
See N. Land, *Victorian workhouse: a study of the
Bromsgrove Union workhouse 1836-1901* (1990).
A. Rate books 1915-26.
B. Min's 1836-1930; parochial ledger 1901-14;
financial statements 1847-75; collectors' monthly
statements 1926-29; sup'an. reg c.1896-1930.
Public Record Office, Kew:
Corres. etc. 1834-1896 [MH 12/13903-27]; staff
reg. 1837-1921 [MH 9/3].

Bromwich, West (Oldbury, Warley).
See under Staffordshire.

Bromyard [9] (Acton Beauchamp, Edvin Loach,
Lower Sapey).
See under Herefordshire.

Cleobury Mortimer [7] (Bayton, Mamble, Rock).
See under Shropshire.

Droitwich [11].
A. Rate book (St. Andrew's) 1898-9; receipt and
exp. book (St. Peter's) etc. 1836-47.
B. Min's 1836-1922; ledger 1836-1921; parochial
ledger 1848-1927; service reg. c.1896-early C20;
overseers' receipts and exp. 1885-1905; health/diet
papers 1687-1974 (sic).
Public Record Office, Kew:
Corres. etc. 1837-1896 [MH 12/13930-56]; staff
reg. 1837-1921 [MH 9/6].

Dudley [1] (formerly Worcs.).
See under Staffordshire.

Evesham [17] (partly Glos.).
A. Reg. of children 1901-30; births reg. 1914-44;
deaths reg. 1866-1914; servants' reg. 1920's;
affiliation book etc. 1830-42; rate book 1856.
B. PLC etc. orders 1836-51, 1924; Guardians'
photo 1929; deeds 1891-1955; conveyance 1879;
SAC byelaws 1880-1900.
Public Record Office, Kew:
Corres. etc. 1834-1896 (missing 1848-51) [MH
12/13997-14013]; staff reg. 1837-1921 [MH 9/6].

Kidderminster [5] (partly Staffs., Shrops.)
(** indicates also available on microfilm at)
Kidderminster Library.
A. Appr. indentures, mostly C19; rate books
(Wolverley) 1924-5; deaths reg.** 1866-84, 1895-
1919; creed reg's late C19-1918; children's home
creed reg. 1915-36; adm. and discharge reg.** 1904-
31 and 1910-41 (sic); creed and inmates reg., mid
C19-20; relief order book (n.d.); discharge book
1895-1904; appl./ report book 1912-3; school fees
receipt and exp. book 1886-1902; relief order book
1908-9; infants reg. 1909-29; Upr Arley assessment
schedule 1839; valuation lists (Broome 1879-97,
Chaddesley Corbett 1879-1913 (+ rate book, n.d.),
Rushock 1887-97); marriage notice book 1837-56.
B. Min's 1836-1928; C'tee min's: Assessment 1862-
1927, W'h. Extension 1881-86, Boarding-out 1910-
29; parochial ledgers 1847-1909; financial
statements 1879-1910; House C'tee reports and
master's report and journal 1914-30; PLC order
1836; sup'an. reg. c.1896-1920; overseers' receipt
and exp. book 1921-27; deeds etc. 1891-1955; reg.
of contracts (n.d.); letter books 1836-61; PLB letters
1836-52; Guardians' attendance reg. 1878-94;
wages receipt book 1929-35; rate return 1904-5;
order check book (sic) 1908; pauper classification
book 1894-1910; relieving officer's voucher list 1900-
06; weekly returns 1913-4, 1929-30; Kidderminster
Infirmary annual reports** 1870-1932.
Public Record Office, Kew:
Corres. etc. 1834-1896 [MH 12/14016-37]; staff
reg. 1837-1921 [MH 9/9].

Kings Norton [3] (partly Warws., Staffs.;
amalgamated with **Birmingham** 1910-11).
Birmingham Central Library (Archives):
A. Vac. reg's (King's Norton 1878-1921, Edgbaston
1880-1918, Harborne 1893-1900, Smethwick 1918-
1922); returns of infant deaths: King's Norton 1872-
1922, Edgbaston 1878-1922, Harborne 1878-1907,
Smethwick 1908-1923; casuals adm. and discharge
reg. 1901; removal orders from Birmingham and
other parishes 1823-27; out relief list 1851; Cottage
Homes reg's (closed for 100 years): children 1887-
1924, deaths 1901-46.
B. Min's 1836-1912; 'various' c'tee and sub-c'tee
min's; relieving officer's appl. book 1849.
Public Record Office, Kew:
Corres. etc. 1834-1896 [MH 12/14039-74]; staff
reg. 1837-1921 [MH 9/9].

Ledbury [14] (West Malvern, Mathon).
See under Herefordshire.

Martley [10].
B. Min's 1863-1917, 1926-30; deeds etc. 1777-
1876; valuation list (Leigh) (n.d.); reg. of officers
and service reg's late C19-20; ac's (Shelsey
Beauchamp)1848-70; RSA min's 1872-82; w'h.
drainage plan 1895; Union division 1899.
Public Record Office, Kew:
Corres. etc. 1834-1896 [MH 12/14079-100]; staff
reg. 1837-1921 [MH 9/11].

Worcestershire continued

Newent [18] (Redmarley d'Abitot, Staunton).
See under Gloucestershire.

Pershore [16].
  A. Creed reg. 1907-30; reg. of infants 1921-30.
  B. Min's 1835-1925; C'tee min's: SAC 1877-87,
Assessment 1863-77, Boarding-out 1912-30,
House 1896-1914; PLC orders etc. 1845;
overseers' ac's book 1832-1909; receipts and exp.
1836-45; insurance policy 1882; bonds 1882, 1892;
salaries' reg. 1920's; stat. abstracts 1837-53;
dietary sheets etc. 1687 (sic)-1974; w'h. ac's 1846;
orders to pay from poor rate 1845-47; ledgers 1835-
1928; letter books 1885-1908; Guardians'
attendance reg. 1899-1930; reports of House c'tee
1914-29; parochial ledger 1847-80.
  Public Record Office, Kew:
  Corres. etc. 1834-1896 (missing 1840-47) [MH
12/14103-14]; staff reg. 1837-1921 [MH 9/13].

Shipston on Stour [21] (Batsford, Blockley,
Shipston on Stour, Tidmington, Tredington).
See under Warwickshire.

Solihull [4] (Yardley).
See under Warwickshire,

Stourbridge [2] (partly Staffs., Shrops.).
  Staffordshire Record Office, Stafford:
  A. Out-relief order books 1870-1929; removal
orders, Cradley, 1843-44; w'h. adm. and discharge
books 1842-92 (vagrants 1870-89); deaths reg.
1868-87; appr. reg. 1846-88; indoor relief lists
1837-92; creed reg's 1869-1900, relieving officer's
appl. and report books 1837-1929; relief lists,
eceipts and exp. c.1837-1926; vac. reg's 1853-99;
poor rate books 1837-95; valuation lists 1847-97.

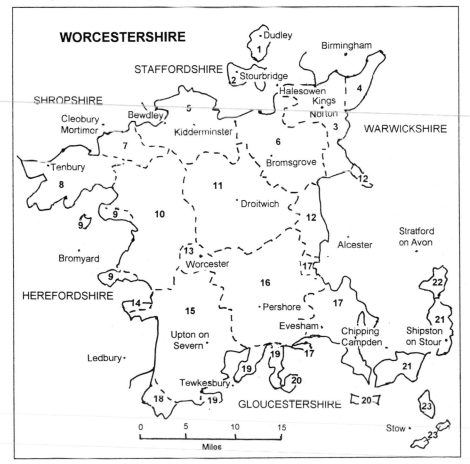

WORCESTERSHIRE

STAFFORDSHIRE

SHROPSHIRE

Dudley
Birmingham
Stourbridge
Halesowen
Kings
Norton
WARWICKSHIRE

Cleobury
Mortimer
Bewdley
Kidderminster
Tenbury
Bromsgrove
Droitwich
Droitwich
Alcester
Stratford
on Avon
Bromyard
Worcester
HEREFORDSHIRE
Pershore
Evesham
Chipping
Campden
Shipston
on Stour
Upton on
Severn
Ledbury
Tewkesbury
GLOUCESTERSHIRE
Stow

0   5   10   15
Miles

Stourbridge *continued*

B. Min's 1836-1929; Finance C'tee min's 1899-1926; other c'tee min's 1893-1927; ledgers 1892-1929; parochial ledgers 1894-1929; financial statements 1895-99; stat. returns 1902-27; pauper classification books 1847-1907; collectors' monthly statements 1876-1911; letter books 1836-98; treasurer's receipts and exp. books, 1867-1930; w'h. master's reports 1866-1915; master's ac's 1873-1905; DMO relief books 1870-1929; collectors' ledgers 1876-1929; contracts for w'h. 1843-1905; appl's for posts of master and matron 1880; statement of population, rateable value, paupers and maintenance 1893; misc. printed returns and reg. of Guardians 1836-82.
Dudley Archives and Local History Service, Coseley.
Some records, as yet unsorted.
Hereford and Worcester Record Office, Worcester:
B. W'h. plans 1902-05; Union boundaries C19; letters, ac's etc, late C19; petition against proposed division (n.d.); min's of Joint C'tee (MOH compensation case) 1896.
Public Record Office, Kew:
Corres. etc. 1834-1896 [MH 12/14134-64]; staff reg. 1837-1921 [MH 9/16].

Stow on the Wold [23] (Daylesford, Evenlode).
See under Gloucestershire.

Stratford on Avon [22] (Alderminster).
See under Warwickshire.

Tenbury [8] (partly Shrops., Heref.).
A. Births reg. 1927-30; deaths reg's 1866-1914, 1927-30; reg. of inmates 1930.
B. Min's 1836-1930; conveyance 1837, 1839.
Public Record Office, Kew:
Corres. etc. 1834-1900 [MH 12/14168-78]; staff reg. 1837-1921 [MH 9/17].

Tewkesbury [19] (Bredon, Bredon's Norton, Chaceley, Conderton, Overbury, Pendock, Teddington).
See under Gloucestershire.

Upton upon Severn [16].
A. Births reg. 1836-66; punishment book 1875-1932; valuation (Birtsmorton) 1826-1908; out relief paid 1836-48; list of non-settled poor 1840.
B. Min's 1835-1903, 1906-26; C'tee min's: House 1926-30, Boarding-out 1920-30; master's report book 1924-28; chaplain's report book 1836-1933; PLC orders 1835; letters 1872; election poster 1850; stat. abstracts 1836-48; sup'an. reg. c.1896-1930; parish expenses 1857; various health papers 1837-57; deeds etc. 1891-1955.
Public Record Office, Kew:
Corres. etc. 1835-1896 [MH 12/14179-99]; staff reg. 1837-1921 [MH 9/17].

West Bromwich see **Bromwich, West**.

Winchcombe [20] (Cutsdean).
See under Gloucestershire.

Worcester [13].
A. Baptisms reg. 1929-71; reg. of children placed out 1926-34; creed reg. 1894-1958; punishment book 1902-58; deaths reg. 1895-early C20; medical relief book 1923-43; reg. of children 1913-1945; relief lists 1911-61; case papers early C20 (index 1920); index to unemployment appl's 1921-1923; collector's receipt and exp. book 1838-48.
B. Min's 1917-30; C'tee min's: Finance 1919-30, House 1926-48, Building 1926-30, Settlement and maintenance 1926-30, Boarding-out 1923-30, Cottage Homes 1926-37, Relief 1926-37 (with agenda book etc. 1926-30, and various others 1923-30; Service reg. 1895-40; ac's book (poor fund) 1910-17; map of Union farm (n.d.); petitions against consecration of burial ground (n.d.); cottage homes reg'ns 1894; chaplain's report book 1893-1948; summary of day books 1929-53; weekly returns 1928-51; requisition books 1929-48; visitors' book 1918-33 (and inspection books 1925-51); Ladies C'tee visiting book 1922-59; receipt and exp. ac's book 1923-45; receipt and exp. books 1929-46; necessaries ac's 1926-28; various clothing ac's 1920-59; garden ac's book 1913-60; MO's report books 1920-56.
Public Record Office, Kew:
Corres. etc. 1834-1896 [MH 12/14202-28]; staff reg. 1837-1921 [MH 9/19].

YORKSHIRE: EAST RIDING and YORK

Unless shown otherwise, records are at *Humberside Record Office, Beverley.*

Beverley [30].
B. Min's 1836-39, 1866-74, 1878-82, 1890-98, 1901-30; Assessment C'tee min's 1887-1905; ledgers 1921-30; reg'ns: punishment of inmates 1914, bathing 1914.
Public Record Office, Kew:
Corres. etc. 1834-1896 [MH 12/14232-53]; staff reg. 1837-1921 [MH 9/2]

Bridlington [23].
A. Reg. of infants 1909-20.
B. Min's 1836-1930; C'tee min's: Assessment 1862-1927, Visiting 1896-1908, 1921-30, Local relief 1914-19; ledgers 1836-1930; summaries of valuation lists 1875-1927; relieving officer's receipt and exp. book 1916-18; reg. of lodging houses 1888-9; Guardians' declarations of acceptance of office 1894-1928; reg. of overseers 1921-26; fortnightly returns of relief provided 1927-29; misc. returns (pauper lunatics, rentals, boarded-out children etc.) 1911-30.
Public Record Office, Kew:
Corres. etc. 1834-1896 [MH 12/14256-70]; staff reg. 1837-1921 [MH 9/3].

Driffield [22].
A. Births reg. 1800-1950; deaths reg. 1866-1947; reg. of seclusion 1923-48; Children's Home creed ledger 1915-48; relief order book 1835-38.
B. Min's 1836-1930 (missing 1913); C'tee min's (Visiting, Finance, Children's Home, Boarding-out, House) 1910-26; Assessment C'tee min's 1875-97; ledgers 1837-1912; highway districts stock and stores ac's 1896-1900; letter books 1836-37, 1889-90; mental defective visiting book 1918-26; plans and spec's for w'h., n.d.; reg'ns re. bathing 1914.
Public Record Office, Kew:
Corres. etc. 1834-1896 [MH 12/14272-89]; staff reg. 1837-1921 [MH 9/6].

Escrick Out Relief (see also under **York**).
B. Min's 1909-24; ledgers 1906-30; pauper classification book 1905-07.

Howden [29].
A. Births and deaths reg's 1914-48; inmates' property reg. 1925-47.
B. Min's 1837-48, 1851-58, 1861-69, 1873-78, 1882-1930; letter book 1842-50; ledgers 1922-30.
Public Record Office, Kew:
Corres. etc. 1834-1896 [MH 12/14291-305]; staff reg. 1837-1921 [MH 9/9].

Kingston upon Hull [46] (Incorporation from 1698).
Kingston upon Hull City Record Office:
A. Annual ward assessments and pension lists 1692-1730; adm. and discharge books 1729-59, 1842-48; reg. of parish appr's 1802-44; poor rate assessments 1724-50, 1820.

B. Min's (Board and c'tees) 1698-1750, 1907-30; ledgers 1894-1930; salary receipt books 1901-04; staff service reg's 1900-36.
Public Record Office, Kew:
Corres. etc. 1847-1896 [MH 12/14306-29]; staff reg. 1837-1921 [MH 9/9].

Malton [20].
See under Yorkshire North Riding.

Norton Out-Relief.
B. Min's 1894-1928; Finance C'tee min's 1904-28; ledgers 1895-1902, 1906-08, 1912-30.

Patrington [33].
A. Pauper offence book 1847-98; births and deaths reg. 1914-47; inventory of property of deceased inmates 1924-46.
B. Master's half-yearly report book 1914-41; ledger 1927-30.
Public Record Office, Kew:
Corres. etc. 1834-1896 [MH 12/14333-43]; staff reg. 1837-1921 [MH 9/13].

Pocklington [21].
A. Adm. and discharge reg's 1852-1964 (30 year closure); relieving officers' receipt and exp. 1855-6, 1860; indoor relief lists 1853-1949; valuation lists 1866-79; reg's: births 1887-1944, deaths 1887-1914, persons 1898-1908, infants 1898-1908, inmates 1903-50, persons receiving reward 1908-28, servants and appr's 1920-32, mechanical restraint 1890-1947; offence and punishment book 1914-40; parochial land tax assessment book c.1904; parochial non-resident relief list 1848-51, weekly out-door relief lists 1836-40, 1845, 1850, 1855-6, 1860, 1865, 1870, 1875, 1880-1, 1885, 1890, 1905, 1910; record of seclusion 1914-47; Children's Home reg. and indoor relief list 1912-32; list of subscribers 1926; reg. of successful vac's 1853-70.
B. Min's 1836-1930; C'tee min's: Assessment 1862-82, 1888-1927, Building 1896-97, House 1923-28, Boarding-out 1910-31; ledgers 1839-41, 1851-62, 1867-70, 1877-81, 1883-1909, 1923-30; SAC parochial ledgers 1893-1900; weekly out-door receipt and exp. 1837-51; newscuttings 1882-1930; letter books 1866-1906; visitors' book (lunatics in w'h.) 1909-23; master's reports and journals 1853-56; treasurer's receipt and exp. 1836-48; fortnightly returns 1925-27; matron's report book 1925-47; visitors' book 1926-48; reg'ns re. allowances, bathing etc. 1915.
Public Record Office, Kew:
Corres. etc. 1834-1896 [MH 12/14344-56]; staff reg. 1837-1921 [MH 9/13]

Scarborough [13].
See under Yorkshire North Riding.

Sculcoates [31] (partly Yorks. N.R.).
Kingston upon Hull City Record Office:
B. Min's 1837-1930; letting of property 1922-30; financial records, ledgers: general 1840-1928, collectors' 1929-30, treasurers' 1904-28, parochial

Yorkshire East Riding: Sculcoates *continued*

1926-7, relief repayment 1915-25, Cottage Homes 1898, staff service 1895-1927.
Public Record Office, Kew:
Corres. etc. 1835-1896 [MH 12/14358-82]; staff reg. 1837-1921 [MH 9/15].

Selby [28].
See under Yorkshire West Riding.

Skirlaugh [32].
B. Min's 1884-90, 1903-06, 1909-11; Assessment C'tee min's 1862-1914; letter book 1888-89; LGB letters 1897-1904; Order for formation of PLU 1837.
Public Record Office, Kew:
Corres. etc. 1836-1896 [MH 12/14384-95]; staff reg. 1837-1921 [MH 9/15].

York: Huggate (a Gilbert Union).
Borthwick Institute of Historical Research, York:
B. Foundation deed 1786.

York [19] (PLU, comprising the city of York and three rural out-relief unions: **Flaxton** (N.R.), **Escrick** (E.R.) and **Bishopthorpe** (W.R.)).
City of York Archives, York:
A. Appl. and report books: city 1837-76 (gaps), 1882, 1905 (west) with vagrants 1848-67, rural 1879-80, 1884; abstracts: city 1840-45, 1847-8, rural 1843-4; relief order books: city 1849-50, 1901-2, 1910-1, 1913-18, 1920-30, rural 1848-53, Flaxton 1901-03; outdoor relief weekly lists: city 1837-1929 (gaps), rural 1879; paupers' case papers 1884-1913; settlement corres. 1911-30 (indexed); creed reg's 1889-1930; adm. and discharge reg. 1880-82; index to adm. and discharge reg's 1889-99; reg. of paupers relieved singly 1907; reg. of indoor cases

1911; births and deaths reg's 1886-1930; reg's of appr's (mainly York) 1845-1929; reg. of boys and girls in farm service 1910-14; reg's of children boarded-out 1898-1920; reg. of persons receiving infants under Infant Life Protection Act: York 1902-10; relieving officer's report book on children boarded-out with foster parents: York 1903-05, Flaxton 1905; reg. of proceedings for enforcing school attendance: Flaxton 1896-1902; vac. reg's: city 1872-1907, rural 1872-1907 (1886 missing).
B. Min's (York) 1837-1930 (also c'tee min's); min's (Flaxton) 1904-29; letter books (York) 1837-1930; ac's and ledgers 1837-1929.
North Yorkshire Record Office, Northallerton:
A. Relief book 1841; appl. and report books 1841, 1871.
B. Bishopthorpe: min's 1903-05, ledger 1921-30; Flaxton: min's 1900-04.
See also under **Escrick**, above.
Borthwick Institute of Historical Research, York (all material contained in parish records and therefore only summarised here):
A. Paupers relieved and vaccinated (St. Mary Castlegate) 1846-7; St. Michael le Belfrey: lists of paupers 1833-72; rate books, various, C19; lists of paupers relieved, and settlement papers C18-19; valuations (Amotherby 1877, Appleton le Street 1879, Flaxton 1837, 1845).
B. Overseer's ac's and assessments 1744-1872; overseers' ac's, various, C18-20; settlement papers, C18-19.
Public Record Office, Kew:
Corres. etc. 1840-1896 (missing 1891) [MH 12/14396-425]; staff reg. 1837-1921 [MH 9/19].

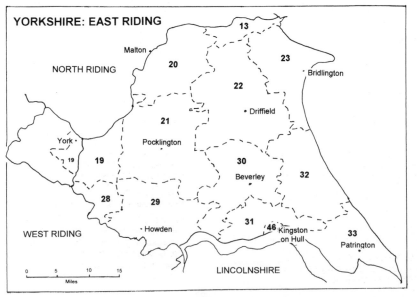

YORKSHIRE: EAST RIDING

13

Malton

20

23

NORTH RIDING

Bridlington

22

Driffield

21

York

Pocklington

19 19

30

Beverley

32

28 29

31

46 Kingston on Hull

33

Patrington

WEST RIDING

Howden

0   5   10   15
Miles

LINCOLNSHIRE

YORKSHIRE: NORTH RIDING

Unless shown otherwise, records are at
North Yorkshire County Record Office,
Northallerton.

Aysgarth [47] (1869 on).
B. Min's 1869-87, 1892-1930; Assessment C'tee min's 1869-1927.
Public Record Office, Kew:
Corres. etc. 1834-1896 [MH 12/14428-35]; staff reg. 1837-1921 [MH 9/1].

Bainbridge [47] (Gilbert Union to 1869, then see Aysgarth).
No records known.

Bedale [45].
Records unsorted, unavailable to the public.
Public Record Office, Kew:
Corres. etc. 1835-1900 (missing 1855- Aug. 1871) [MH 12/14444-53]; staff reg. 1837-1921 [MH 9/2].

Darlington [3] (Barton, Cleasby, Cliffe, Croft, Dalton upon Tees, Over Dinsdale, Eryholme, Girsby, Manfield, Newton Morrell, Stapleton).
See under Co. Durham.

Easingwold [18] (partly Co. Durham).
A. Adm. and discharge books 1882-94, 1900-13, 1922-31; births reg. 1867-1931, deaths reg. 1866 1931; creed reg. 1867-1930.
B. Min's 1837-1904; list of investments 1930.
Public Record Office, Kew:
Corres. etc. 1834-1896 (missing 1843-47, 1854-66) [MH 12/14436-43]; staff reg. 1837-1921 [MH 9/6].

Flaxton out-relief union. See under East Riding.

Guisborough [6].
Cleveland County Archives Department, Middlesbrough.
A. Adm. and discharge reg's 1837-1930.
B. Min's and ledgers 1837-1930.
Public Record Office, Kew:
Corres. etc. 1834-1896 (missing 1878) [MH 12/14454-80], staff reg. 1837-1921 [MH 9/7].

Helmsley (Blackmoor) [11].
B. Min's 1837-67.
Public Record Office, Kew:
Corres. etc. 1835-1900 [MH 12/14483-92]; staff reg. 1837-1921 [MH 9/8].

Kirkby Moorside (from 1848, formed out of Helmsley and Pickering).
Records unsorted, unavailable to the public.
Public Record Office, Kew:
Corres. etc. 1848-1900 [MH 12/14494-501]; staff reg. 1848-1921 [MH 9/9].

Leyburn [8].
Records (very few) unsorted, unavailable to the public.
Public Record Office, Kew:
Corres. etc. 1834-1896 [MH 12/14502-12]; staff reg. 1837-1921 [MH 9/10].

Malton [20] (partly East Riding).
A. Outdoor relief list 1848-51.
Public Record Office, Kew:
Corres. etc. 1834-1896 [MH 12/14513-30]; staff reg. 1837-1921 [MH 9/11].

Middlesbrough (from 1875, formed out of Stockton).
Cleveland County Archives Department, Middlesbrough.
A. Adm. and discharge reg's 1894-1930.
B. Min's 1875-1930.
Public Record Office, Kew:
Corres. etc. 1875-1896 [MH 12/14533-55]; staff reg. 1875-1921 [MH 9/11].

Northallerton [9].
A. Adm. and discharge reg's 1837-86
B. Min's 1837-1930; SAC min's 1895-1903.
Public Record Office, Kew:
Corres. etc. 1839-1896 [MH 12/14560-73]; staff reg. 1837-1921 [MH 9/12].

Ouseburn, Great (Gilbert Union).
See under Yorkshire West Riding.

Pickering [12].
A. Adm. and discharge books 1837-1949 (gaps); births reg. 1843-1931; deaths reg. 1837-1931; creed reg. 1900-17
B. Min's 1837-1930.
Public Record Office, Kew:
Corres. etc. 1835-1896 [MH 12/14575-86]; staff reg. 1837-1921 [MH 9/13].

Reeth [2].
B. Min's 1840-56.
Public Record Office, Kew:
Corres. etc. 1835-1896 [MH 12/14587-94]; staff reg. 1837-1921 [MH 9/14].

Richmond [2].
B. Min's 1837-78, 1882-1930; w'h. plans 1841.
Public Record Office, Kew:
Corres. etc. 1834-1896 (missing 1846-7, 1891-2) [MH 12/14595-609]; staff reg. 1837-1921 [MH 9/14].

Ripon [50].
See under Yorkshire West Riding.

Scarborough [13] (partly East Riding).
B. Min's 1837-84; Children's Home C'tee min's 1920-30.
Public Record Office, Kew:
Corres. etc. 1834-1896 [MH 12/14610-28]; staff reg. 1837-1921 [MH 9/15].

Sculcoates [31].
See under Yorkshire East Riding.

Stockton [4] (West Acklam, Ingleby Barwick, Castle and Kirk Leavington, Linthorpe, Maltby, Middlesbrough, Picton, Stainton, Thornaby, High and Low Worsall, Yarm).
See under Co. Durham.

Yorkshire North Riding continued

Stokesley [5].
Records unsorted, unavailable to the public.
Public Record Office, Kew:
Corres. etc. 1834-1896 [MH 12/14631-38]; staff reg. 1837-1921 [MH 9/16].

Teesdale [1] (Barforth, Barningham, Boldron, Bowes, Brignall, Cotherstone, Egglestone Abbey, Gilmonby, Holwick, Hope, Hunderthwaite, Hutton Magna, Lartington, Lunedale, Mickleton, Ovington, Rokeby, Romandkirk, Scargill, Startforth, Wycliffe with Thorpe).
See under Co. Durham.

Thirsk [10].
B. Min's 1909-30; Boarding-out C'tee min's 1915-30.
Public Record Office, Kew:
Corres. etc. 1834-1896 [MH 12/14639-54]; staff reg. 1837-1921 [MH 9/17].

Whitby [7].
B. Min's 1837-81; SAC min's 1877-1903.
Public Record Office, Kew:
Corres. etc. 1834-1896 (missing June 1887 - June 1890) [MH 12/14656-72]; staff reg. 1837-1921 [MH 9/18].

York [19].
See under Yorkshire East Riding.

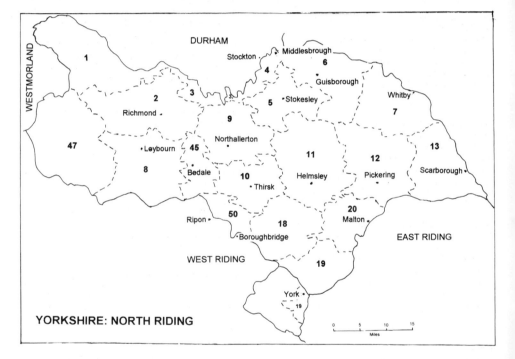

YORKSHIRE: NORTH RIDING

YORKSHIRE: WEST RIDING

Barnsley [50].
Barnsley Archive Service:
B. Min's 1850-1930; C'tee min's: SAC 1877-1902, House 1899-1930, Boarding-out 1901-30, Finance 1916-30.
Barnsley Central Library:
A. Printed ac's 1854 (incl. names of paupers).
B. Printed ac's 1879-80.
Wakefield Library (Local Studies and Archives):
A. Lists of poor 1857-60.
B. Ac's 1855-6.
Public Record Office, Kew:
Corres. etc. 1834-96 [MH 12/14674-704], staff reg. 1837-1921 [MH 9/2].

Barwick in Elmet [50] (Gilbert Union to 1869; then see **Tadcaster**).
Yorkshire Archaeological Society, Leeds:
Ac's book 1822-48, with resolutions 1848-59.
Leeds District Archives:
A. Incorporation rates 1848.
Public Record Office, Kew:
Corres. etc. 1834-1869 [MH 12/15548-49]; staff reg. 1837-69 [MH 9/2].

Bierley, North [50] (from 1848).
Keighley Reference Library:
A. Orders for boarding-out children 1881-1910; reg. of lunatics 1888-1940, reg. of inmates 1912-39.
B. Min's 1848-1930, C'tee Min's: Assessment 1866-1904, Special 1893-1909, Boarding-out and Building 1901-30, Infirmary 1904-30, House 1905-29, Finance and Children's 1908-30, LGB corres. 1893-1928; Registrar General corres. 1904-14; PLC orders 1847-1908; ledgers 1919-25; ac's books 1907-55; sup'an. 1910-30; cash ac's book (coke for w'h.) 1914-76.
Bradford Central Library (Local Studies):
A. List of paupers (printed) 1894.
B. Year books (printed) 1879-1901 (gaps).
Public Record Office, Kew:
Corres. etc. 1848-96 [MH 12/14768-820]; staff reg. 1848-1921 [MH 9/12].

Bishopthorpe out-relief union. See East Riding.

Bradford [27].
Bradford District Archives
(records containing personal information are closed for 100 years, though specific items may be made available with a letter of authority from the Welfare Dept. of Bradford Metropolitan District Council):
A. Employment records 1862-1930; adm. and discharge books 1857-1930; birth and death reg's 1838-1930; creed reg's 1859-1930; punishment books 1888-1930; reg. of adopted children 1899-1930.
B. Various min's 1837-1930; financial records 1838-1931; corres. 1837-77; orders 1837-67; inventory books 1910-30; master's report books 1913-28; trinket books 1903-30; pauper lunatic reports etc. 1864-1929;

Bradford Central Library (Local Studies):
A. Out-door paupers (printed) 1878.
B. Printed min's (incl. c'tees) 1907-30 (gaps); year books 1873-1920 (gaps).
Public Record Office, Kew:
Corres. etc. 1834-96 [MH 12/14720-63]; staff reg. 1837-1921 [MH 9/3].

Bramley [50] (1862 on).
Leeds District Archives (at least one week's notice is required for production of these records):
A. Rate books 1844-1921; valuation books 1863-1922; misc. rate collections 1872-76; reg. of contribution orders 1877-99; reg. of maintenance orders 1900-25; reg. of ag'mts of contributors 1909-25; foster parents' undertakings 1908-23; ag'mts for payment of maintenance c.1887-1923; settlement and removal reg's 1879-1901; Wortley tithe map and award 1846; draft valuation book 1906.
B. Min's 1901-26; corres. 1900-25; various 1845-53; overseers' and surveyors' ac's 1854-61; assessment papers c.1900-20; poor rate ledger overseers' balance sheets 1905-11; collector's monthly statement book 1868-76; ag'mts with other Unions 1869-70; list of Guardians and officers 1902-21; Guardians' declarations 1894-1919; Poor Law maps and plans 1910-14.
Public Record Office, Kew:
Corres. etc. 1863-96 [MH 12/14707-19]; staff reg. 1863-1921 [MH 9/3].

Burnley (Cliviger).
See under Lancashire

Carlton [50] (Gilbert Union to 1869).
Leeds District Archives (see **Bramley** above):
B. MO's book 1860s.
Public Record Office, Kew:
Corres. etc. 1835-69 [MH 12/15286-88]; staff reg. 1837-69 [MH 9/4].

Clitheroe [15] (Bashall Eaves, Bolton by Bowland, Bowland Forest, West Bradford, Easington, Gisburn, Gisburn Forest, Grindleton, Horton, Middop, Great Mitton, Newsholme, Newton, Paythorne, Rimington, Sawley, Slaidbur, Waddington).
See under Lancashire.

Dewsbury [35].
Kirklees District Archives, Huddersfield:
A. Appl. for relief and tabulations 1906-7; relief order books (incl. c'tee min's 1912-30); medical returns 1915-29.
B. Min's 1837-42; calculations on loans 1892-1923; RSA Mirfield parochial c'tee min's 1871-73.
Public Record Office, Kew:
Corres. etc. 1834-96 [MH 12/14830-82]; staff reg. 1837-1921 [MH 9/82].

Doncaster [42] (partly Yorks. N.R. and Notts.).
No locallly held records have survived.
Public Record Office, Kew:
Corres. etc. 1834-96 [MH 12/14903-31]; staff reg. 1837-1921 [MH 9/6].

Yorkshire West Riding *continued*

Ecclesall Bierlow [38] (partly Derbys.).
Sheffield Archives:
Restricted access: * = closed for 75 years;
• = closed for 100 years; from date of last entry;
searches will be made for specific entries by
Archives staff.
A. Adm. (or creed) reg's 1883-1906, *1907-28;
asylum adm. reg's •1920-28; reg's of inmates 1904-
15, *1915-31; creed reg's 1902-31 (males to 1923);
deaths reg's •1903-31; births reg's •1898-1929.
Public Record Office, *Kew:*
Corres. etc. 1834-96 [MH 12/14938-52]; staff reg.
1837-1921 [MH 9/6].

Goole [44] (partly Lincs. Pts. Lindsey).
Humberside Archive Service, *Beverley:*
B. Min's 1837-1930; ledgers 1837-1927.
Public Record Office, *Kew:*
Corres. etc. 1834-96 [MH 12/14954-72]; staff reg.
1837-1921 [MH 9/7].

Great Ouseburn see **Ouseburn, Great.**
Great Preston see **Preston, Great.**

Halifax (township, pre-1837).
Calderdale District Archives, *Halifax:*
A. Settlement, appr. and bastardy papers 1673-
1749; index to names of persons mentioned in PL
papers 1672-1842.

Halifax [26].
Calderdale District Archives, *Halifax:*
A. Out-relief books, listing recipients, 1895 (wards:
Northowram (western division), Skircoat,
Southowram, West, unspecified), n.d. (East, South,
several unspecified).
B. Min's 1837-41; ledgers 1835-39, 1857-1925;
treasurer's ac's 1907-13; salaries and wages 1912-
24 (gaps); hospital nursing staff wages 1905-10; PL
Hospital wages 1914, 1918; St. Luke's Hospital
wages 1922; stat. portion book 1930; misc. corres.
re. working of PL in Halifax, rateable values etc.
1866-97; misc. ag'mts and corres. 1885-1929; Union
w'h.: plans 1862-70 and n.d.; New w'h. infirmary or
St. Luke's War Hospital: building and maintenance
contracts 1896-1923; vac. officer's contracts 1904-
28; DMO's contract 1917-23; probationer nurses'
ag'mts 1923-29.
Calderdale Central Library, *Halifax:*
B. Min's (printed) 1898, 1902-30; commemorative
booklet 1930.
Public Record Office, *Kew:*
Corres. etc. 1834-96 [MH 12/14974-15029]; staff
reg. 1837-1921 [MH 9/8].

Hemsworth [50] (1850 on).
West Yorkshire Archive Service H.Q., *Wakefield:*
A. Outdoor relief order books 1873-1930; relief
books 1906-31; Stansfield View w'h.: infirmary adm.
and discharge reg. 1879-1954; deaths reg. 1914-36;
indoor relief lists 1922-30.
B. Min's 1860-1911; letter books 1872-1929;
corres. 1894-c.1930; ledger 1850-1901; receipts and

exp's 1891-1930; Stansfield View w'h. min's 1911-
32.
Public Record Office, *Kew:*
Corres. etc. 1850-96 [MH 12/15041-55]; staff reg.
1837-1921 [MH 9/8].

Holbeck [50] (1862 on).
Leeds District Archives:
A. Beeston tithe award 1847; births reg. 1863-
1914; deaths reg. 1862-1914; reg. of lunatics in w'h.
1883-1914.
B. Min's 1869-74; LGB letters etc. 1884-87;
amalgamation enquiry 1884; insurance policies
1870-1908; dissolution papers 1925-6; in letters
1877-8; Beeston township map 1857.
Leeds Central Library:
B. Year book (printed) 1924-5.
Public Record Office, *Kew:*
Corres. etc. 1834-1862 [MH 12/15056-62]; staff
reg. 1837-1921 [MH 9/8].

Huddersfield [34].
Kirklees District Archives, *Huddersfield:*
A. Printed lists of persons relieved 1875-1913.
B. Min's 1837-1930 (printed from 1912);
Assessment C'tee min's 1862-1927 (and for Upper
Agbrigg 1927-44); ac's 1862-1930; ledgers 1928-32;
LGB sanctions 1877-1914; deeds etc. 1840-1947;
corres. 1849-1943; ag'mts 1844-1947; plans C19-
20.
Huddersfield Central Library:
B. Ac's (printed) 1861-66, 1878; list of Guardians
1879; Guardians' handbook 1895.
Public Record Office, *Kew:*
Corres. etc. 1834-96 [MH 12/15063-131]; staff reg.
1837-1921 [MH 9/9].

Hunslet [50] (from 1862).
Leeds District Archives:
A. Tithe map and award 1845.
B. Poor Law maps and plans 1862-1922.
Leeds Central Library:
B. Printed year books 1882-1925 (gaps).
Public Record Office, *Kew:*
Corres. etc. 1862-96 [MH 12/15141-55]; staff reg.
1837-1921 [MH 9/9].

Keighley [24].
Keighley Reference Library:
A. Non-resident and non-settled poor ledgers
1861-74.
B. Min's 1837-1930; C'tee min's 1877-1904; letter
books 1837-1910; LGB returns 1886-1912; lists of
Guardians etc. 1839, 1843-1916, 1920-1; ledgers
1884-1923; parochial ledgers 1876-1910; treasurer's
ac's 1896-1910; financial statements 1879-1919;
poor rate returns 1875-1930; cash book 1914-22;
non-settled poor ledgers 1885-1910.
Wakefield Library (Local Studies and Archives):
B. Printed return and reports 1842.
Public Record Office, *Kew:*
Corres. etc. 1834-96 [MH 12/15158-95]; staff reg.
1837-1921 [MH 9/9].

Yorkshire West Riding *continued*

Knaresborough (pre-1854).
Yorkshire Archaeological Society, Leeds:
Master's day book, 1788-91.

Knaresborough [50] (from 1854).
North Yorkshire County Record Office,
Northallerton:
B. Min's 1854-1930; ledgers 1854-72, 1925-30;
Visiting and Special C'tee's min's 1893-1917.
Public Record Office, Kew:
Corres. etc. ?1834-96 [MH 12/15201-21]; staff reg.
?1837-1921 [MH 9/9].

Leeds [50] (Guardians 1844-69, PLU 1869-1912,
Par. 1912 on).
Leeds District Archives:
A. Reg. of emigrant children 1888-95; relief order
books 1845-1945 (incl adm. and discharge book
1843-47, and vagrants' adm. and discharge book
1902-3); medical relief books 1875-1939; settlement
records 1869-1937; case books 1869-1948; reg. of
adoptions 1895-1948; reg. of bastardy 1844-1930;
reg. of objections to property owners 1873-82;
reception orders for pauper lunatics 1877-1929;
appr. indentures 1849-1923; valuation lists 1837-
1930.
B. Min's 1844-1930; ledgers ('ac's') 1818-1933
(incl. overseers of Leeds township); letter books
1845-1935 (incl. boarding-out and emigration 1887-
1919); out letters 1849-1937; returns made to
Guardians 1848-1932; Boarding-out C'tee report
and returns 1895-1948, reg. of appointments 1864-
98, 1908-28; accepted tenders 1848-1900; PLC,
PLB, LGB orders 1844-1924; election of Guardians
1888-1915; corres. re. military occupation 1914-10;
property 1857-1946; papers re. amalgamation of
Unions 1860-1927; PL maps and plans 1857-1941.
Leeds Central Library:
A. Paupers relieved (printed) 1884.
B. Min's (printed) 1907-30; newscuttings 1891-
1943; year books 1898-1930; Jewish BG annual
reports 1893-4, 1919-20, 1922-3.
Public Record Office, Kew:
Corres. etc. ?1834-96 [MH 12/15224-70]; staff reg.
?1837-1921 [MH 9/10].

Otley [50].
No locally held records known.
Public Record Office, Kew:
No MH 12 refs.; staff reg. 1837-1921 [MH 9/12].

Ouseburn, Great [50] (Gilbert Union to 1854; then
PLU) (partly Yorks. N.R.).
North Yorkshire County Record Office,
Northallerton:
B. Min's 1898-1930.
Public Record Office, Kew:
Corres. etc. 1855-96 [MH 12/15275-85]; staff reg.
?1837-1921 [MH 9/12].

Pateley Bridge [17].
North Yorkshire County Record Office,
Northallerton:
B. Min's 1837-88.
Public Record Office, Kew:
Corres. etc. 1835-96 [MH 12/15289-303]; staff reg.
1837-1921 [MH 9/13].

Penistone (formed from **Wortley** 1849).
Barnsley Archive Service:
A. Vac. reg's: High Hoyland 1901-31, Cawthorne
district 1 1898-1927, Penistone district 3 1898-1931.
Public Record Office, Kew:
Corres. etc. 1849-52 [MH 12/15304-19]; staff reg.
?1837-1921 [MH 9/13].

Pontefract [50] (?from 1862).
West Yorkshire Archive Service H.Q., Wakefield:
B. Min's 1907-30; ledger 1926-30.
Public Record Office, Kew:
Corres. etc. ?1834-96 (missing 1882) [MH
12/15321-45]; staff reg. ?1837-1921 [MH 9/13].

Preston, Great [50] (Gilbert Union to 1869).
No locally held records known.
Public Record Office, Kew:
Corres. etc. 1852-69 [MH 12/15350-67]; staff reg.
1837-69 [MH 9/13].

Ripon [50] (from ?1852) (partly Yorks. N.R.).
North Yorkshire County Record Office,
Northallerton:
A. Outdoor relief list 1867-68.
B. SAC min's 1877-96.
Public Record Office, Kew:
No MH 12 refs.; staff reg. 1852-1921 [MH 9/14].

Rotherham [40] (partly Derbys.).
Rotherham Central Library (Archives and Local
Studies):
A. Rotherham w'h.: creed reg's 1883-1932 (missing
1895/6); inmates' relatives (males only) 1887-91,
1911-32 (gaps); reg. of vagrants and remand cases
1921-40; punishment book 1904-14; births reg.
1848-79, 1912-38; counterfoils: notices to coroner of
deaths of persons of unsound mind 1900-33.
B. Min's 1837-1930 (gaps); Assessment C'tee
min's 1890-1913; other c'tee min's from 1909; ledger
1925-26; master's report and journal 1913-48
(gaps); visitors' reports 1926-60; wages 1908-19
(gaps).
Public Record Office, Kew:
Corres. etc. 1834-96 [MH 12/15368-404]; staff reg.
1837-1921 [MH 9/14].

Saddleworth [49] (Gilbert Union to 1853; then
Par./PLU).
No locally held records known.
Public Record Office, Kew:
Corres. etc. 1853-96 (missing 1853-56) [MH
12/15409-17]; staff reg. 1837-1921 [MH 9/15].

Sedbergh [48].
Cumbria Record Office, Kendal:
B. Min's 1894-98, 1906-30; ledgers 1912-30.
Public Record Office, Kew:
Corres. etc. 1837-96 [MH 12/15419-29]; staff reg.
1837-1921 [MH 9/15].

Selby [28] (partly Yorks. E.R.).
North Yorkshire County Record Office,
Northallerton:
A. Deaths reg. 1914-42; reg. of lunatics 1889-1947.
Yorkshire Archaeological Society, Leeds:
B. W'h. ac's 1837.
Public Record Office, Kew:
Corres. etc. 1834-96 [MH 12/15430-45]; staff reg.
1837-1921 [MH 9/15].

Settle [14].
North Yorkshire County Record Office,
Northallerton:
Records unsorted, unavailable to the public.
Yorkshire Archaeological Society, Leeds:
Papers, C19, incl. MoH reports.
Public Record Office, Kew:
Corres. etc. 1834-94 [MH 12/15447-63]; staff reg.
1837-1921 [MH 9/15].

Sheffield [39].
Sheffield Archives:
'Legend has it that the majority of Sheffield Union's
records were destroyed during the blitz when the
former union offices were destroyed.'
B. Min's (printed) 1890-1930 (gaps) (also in *Local*
Studies Library).
Public Record Office, Kew:
Corres. etc. 1834-96 [MH 12/15465-506]; staff reg.
1837-1921 [MH 9/15].

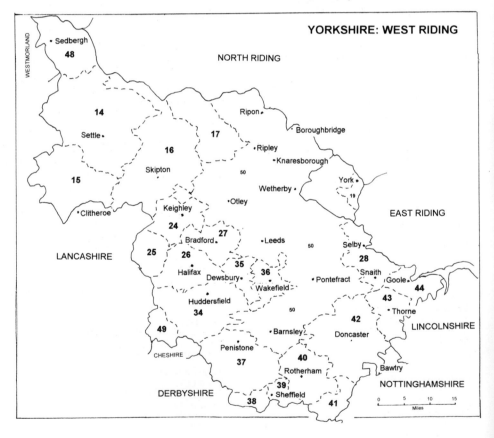

Yorkshire West Riding continued

Skipton [16].
North Yorkshire County Record Office, *Northallerton:*
B. Min's 1906-30 (gaps); Assessment C'tee min's 1901-27.
Skipton Library:
A. Outdoor relief lists 1923-27; emigration of children 1911-13; reg. of foster parents 1916-30; reg. of non-settled and non-resident poor 1924-30; relief order books: western dist. 1893-96, 1902-05, 1909-29, eastern dist. 1902-06, eastern and northern 1919-30; casual paupers adm. and discharged (n.d.); DMO's relief book 1897-1900 (missing).
B. Addingham collector's ac's 1923-27; DMO returns 1921-29; hot water supply 1925-6; Yorkshire vagrancy c'tee 1913-28; financial statement 1927-8; weekly returns of persons in receipt of relief 1920-22; ac's 1921-28; salaries 1921-2; receipts re. boarding-out 1921-2 and re. fostered children (n.d.); appointment of overseers 1901-14, 1917-27; weekly returns form A 1913-30, form B 1928-30; letter books 1903-4, 1907-29; Guardians' attendance reg. 1904-27(?); w'h. alterations 1927-30.
Public Record Office, *Kew:*
Corres. etc. 1834-95 [MH 12/15512-32]; staff reg. 1837-1921 [MH 9/15].

Tadcaster [50] (from 1862).
North Yorkshire County Record Office, *Northallerton:*
B. Min's 1862-67; Assessment C'tee min's 1907-27; ledgers 1862-1930.
Public Record Office, *Kew:*
Corres. etc. 1865-96 [MH 12/15536-47]; staff reg. 1837-1921 [MH 9/17].
See also **Barwick in Elmet**.

Thorne [43] (partly Lincs. Pts. Lindsey).
Doncaster Borough Archives:
B. Min's 1837-42.
Public Record Office, *Kew:*
Corres. etc. 1834-96 [MH 12/15550-64]; staff reg. 1837-1921 [MH 9/17].

Todmorden [25] (partly Lancs.).
Calderdale District Archives, *Halifax:*
A. Adm. and discharge book 1880-82.
B. Min's 1882-1911; letter book 1837-41; w'h. ac's. 1875-79.

Public Record Office, *Kew:*
Corres. etc. 1834-1900 (missing 1845-51, 1856-7, 1876) [MH 12/6272-98]; staff reg. 1837-1921 [MH 9/17].

Wakefield [36].
West Yorkshire Archive Service H.Q., *Wakefield:*
B. Min's 1897-1930; ledger ac's 1930.
Wakefield Library (Local Studies and Archives):
A. 'Several hundreds' of PL records relating to individuals, all listed.
B. Printed min's 1897-1903; ac's 1850; statement of number of paupers relieved 1886, 1889.
Public Record Office, *Kew:*
Corres. etc. 1834-96 [MH 12/15566-608]; staff reg. 1837-1921 [MH 9/18].

Wetherby [50] (from 1861).
Leeds District Archives:
B. Corres. c.1909.
Public Record Office, *Kew:*
Corres. etc. 1861-96 [MH 12/15616-25]; staff reg. 1861-1921 [MH 9/18].

Wharfedale [50] (a Gilbert w'h. established in 1818; PLU from 1861).
Leeds District Archives:
B. Pauper classification book 1876-78; medical book for Carlton w'h. (Otley) 1866-69.
Public Record Office, *Kew:*
Corres. etc. 1861-96 [MH 12/15627-49]; staff reg. 1861-1921 [MH 9/18].

Worksop [41] (North and South Anston, Dinnington, Firbeck, Gildingwells, Harthill with Woodall, Letwell, St. John's with Throapham, Thorpe Salvin, Todwick, Wales, Wallingwells, Woodsetts).
See under Nottinghamshire.

Wortley [37] (see also **Penistone**).
Sheffield Archives:
B. Min's 1838-1929 (printed from 1905); C'tee min's incl. in main min's: Boarding-out from 1915 (gaps), House 1921 only, Mental Deficiency Accommodation 1928-9; SAC 1877-1904; ledger 1923-25.
Public Record Office, *Kew:*
Corres. etc. 1835-96 [MH 12/15655-70]; staff reg. 1837-1921 [MH 9/19].

York [19].
See under Yorkshire East Riding.

ALPHABETICAL LISTING OF UNIONS

Aberaeron, *Cards.*
Abergavenny, *Mon.*
Aberystwyth, *Cards.*
Abingdon, *Berks.*
Albans, St., *Herts.*
Alcester, *Warw.*
Alderbury, *Wilts.*
Alstonfield, *Staffs.*
Alnwick, *Nhmbd.*
Alresford, *Hants.*
Alston, *Cumbs.*
Alton, *Hants.*
Altrincham, *Ches.*
Alverstoke, *Hants.*
Amersham, *Bucks.*
Amesbury, *Wilts.*
Ampthill, *Beds.*
Andover, *Hants.*
Anglesey, *Ang.*
Arrington, *Cambs.*
Arundel, *Sussex*
Asaph, St., *Flints.*
Ash, *Surrey*
Ashbourne, *Dbys.*
Ashby de la Zouch, *Leics.*
Ashford, East, *Kent*
Ashford, West, *Kent*
Ashton, Long, *Som.*
Ashton under Lyne, *Lancs.*
Aston, *Warw*
Atcham, *Salop.*
Atherstone, *Warw.*
Auckland (Bishop's), *Durh.*
Austell, St., *Corn.*
Axbridge, *Som.*
Axminster, *Devon*
Aylesbury, *Bucks.*
Aylesford, North, *Kent*
Aylsham, *Norf.*
Aysgarth, *Yorks. N.R.*

Bainbridge, *Yorks. N.R.*
Bakewell, *Dbys.*
Bala, *Merioneth*
Banbury, *Oxon.*
Bangor, *Caerns.*
Barnet, *Herts.*
Barnsley, *Yorks. W.R.*
Barnstaple, *Devon*
Barrow in Furness, *Lancs.*
Barrow on Soar, *Leics.*
Barton Regis, *Glos.*
Barton upon Irwell, *Lancs.*

Barwick(-in-Elmet), *Yorks. W.R.*
Basford, *Notts.*
Basingstoke, *Hants.*
Bath, *Som.*
Battle, *Sussex*
Beaminster, *Dorset*
Beaumaris, *Caerns.*
Bedale, *Yorks. N.R.*
Bedford, *Beds.*
Bedwelty, *Mon.*
Belford, *Nhmbd.*
Bellingham, *Nhmbd.*
Belper, *Dbys.*
Berkhampstead, *Herts.*
Bermondsey, *London: Surrey*
Berwick-on-Tweed, *Nhmbd.*
Bethnal Green, *London: Middx.*
Beverley, *Yorks. E.R.*
Bicester, *Oxon.*
Bideford, *Devon*
Bierley, North, *Yorks. W.R.*
Diggloowado, *Beds.*
Billericay, *Essex*
Billesden, *Leics.*
Bingham, *Notts.*
Birkenhead, *Ches.*
Birmingham, *Warw.*
Bishops Auckland, *Dur.*
Bishops Stortford, *Herts.*
Blaby, *Leics.*
Blackburn, *Lancs.*
Blandford, *Dorset*
Blean, *Kent*
Blofield, *Norf.*
Blything, *Suff.*
Bodmin, *Corn.*
Bolton, *Lancs.*
Bootle, *Cumbd.*
Bosmere, *Suff.*
Bosworth, Market, *Leics.*
Boston, *Lincs.*
Boughton, Great, *Ches.*
Bourne, *Lincs.*
Bournemouth, *Hants.*
Brackley, *N'hants.*
Bradfield, *Berks.*
Bradford(-on-Avon), *Wilts.*
Bradford, *Yorks. W.R.*
Braintree, *Essex*
Bramley, *Yorks. W.R.*

Brampton, *Cumbd.*
Brecknock, *Brecons.*
Brentford, *Middx.*
Bridge, *Kent*
Bridgend, *Glam.*
Bridgewater, *Som.*
Bridgnorth, *Salop.*
Bridlington, *Yorks. E.R.*
Bridport, *Dorset*
Brighton, *Sussex,*
Brinton, *Norf.*
Bristol, *Glos.*
Brixworth, *N'hants.*
Bromley, *Kent*
Bromsgrove, *Worcs.*
Bromwich, West, *Staffs.*
Bromyard, *Heref.*
Buckingham, *Bucks.*
Bucklow, *Ches.*
Builth, *Brecons.*
Buntingford, *Herts.*
Burnley, *Lancs.*
Burslem, *Staffs.*
Burton-on-Trent, *Staffs.*
Bury, *Lancs.*
Bury St. Edmunds, *Suff.*

Caernarvon, *Caerns.*
Caistor, *Lincs.*
Calne, *Wilts.*
Camberwell, *London: Surrey*
Cambridge, *Cambs.*
Camelford, *Corn.*
Cannock, *Staffs.*
Canterbury, *Kent*
Cardiff, *Glam.*
Cardigan, *Cards.*
Carlisle, *Cumbd.,*
Carlton, *Yorks. W.R.*
Carmarthen, *Carms.*
Carnarvon, *Caerns.*
Castle Ward, *Nhmbd.*
Catherington, *Hants.*
Caton, *Lancs.*
Caxton, *Cambs.*
Cerne, *Dorset*
Chailey, *Sussex*
Chapel en le Frith, *Dbys.*
Chard, *Som.*
Cheadle, *Staffs.*
Chelmsford, *Essex*
Chelsea, *London: Middx.*
Cheltenham, *Glos.*
Chepstow, *Mon.*
Chertsey, *Surrey*

Chester, *Ches.*
Chesterfield, *Dbys.*
Chester-le-Street, *Dur.*
Chesterton, *Cambs.*
Chichester, *Sussex*
Chippenham, *Wilts.*
Chipping Norton, *Oxon.*
Chipping Sodbury, *Glos.*
Chorley, *Lancs.*
Chorlton, *Lancs.*
Christchurch, *Hants.*
Church Stretton, *Salop.*
Cirencester, *Glos.*
Clapham, *London: Surrey*
Clavering, *Norf.*
Claydon, *Suff.*
Cleobury Mortimer, *Salop.*
Clerkenwell, *London: Middx.*
Clifton, *Glos.*
Clitheroe, *Lancs.*
Clun, *Salop.*
Clutton, *Som.*
Cockermouth, *Cumbd.*
Colchester, *Essex*
Columb, St. Major, *Corn.*
Congleton, *Ches.*
Conway, *Caerns.*
Cookham, *Berks.*
Corwen, *Merioneth*
Costord, *Suff.*
Coventry, *Warw.*
Cowbridge, *Glam.*
Cranborne, *Dorset*
Cranbrook, *Kent*
Crediton, *Devon*
Crickhowell, *Brecons.*
Cricklade, *Wilts.*
Croydon, *Surrey*
Cuckfield, *Sussex*

Darlington, *Dur.*
Dartford, *Kent*
Daventry, *N'hants.*
Depwade, *Norf.*
Derby, *Dbys.*
Derby, West, *Lancs.*
Devizes, *Wilts.*
Devonport, *Devon*
Dewsbury, *Yorks. W.R.*
Docking, *Norf.*
Dolgelly, *Merioneth*
Doncaster, *Yorks. W.R.* .
Dorchester, *Dorset*

Dore, *Heref.*
Dorking, *Surrey*
Dover, *Kent*
Downham, *Norf.*
Drayton, *Salop.*
Driffield, *Yorks. E.R.*
Droitwich, *Worcs.*
Droxford, *Hants.*
Dudley, *Staffs.*
Dulverton, *Som.*
Dunmow, *Essex*
Durham, *Dur.*
Dursley, *Glos.*

Easington, *Dur.*
Easingwold, *Yorks. N.R.*
Eastbourne, *Sussex*
East Ashford, *Kent*
East Flegg, *Norf.*
East Grinstead, *Sussex*
Easthampstead, *Brks.*
East Preston, *Sussex*
East Retford, *Notts.*
Eastry, *Kent*
East Stonehouse,
 Devon
East Ward, *Westmd.*
Ecclesall Bierlow,
 Yorks. W R
Edmonton, *Middx.*
Elham, *Kent*
Ellesmere, *Salop.*
Ely, *Cambs.*
Epping, *Essex*
Epsom, *Surrey*
Erpingham, *Norf.*
Eton, *Bucks.*
Evesham, *Worcs.*
Exeter, *Devon*

Faith, St., *Norf.*
Falmouth, *Corn.*
Fareham, *Hants.*
Farnborough, *Hants.*
Farnham, *Surrey*
Faringdon, *Berks.*
Faversham, *Kent*
Festiniog, *Merioneth*
Firle, West, *Sussex*
Flegg, East and West,
 Norf.
Foleshill, *Warw.*
Forden, *Mont.*
Fordingbridge, *Hants.*
Forehoe, *Norf.*
Forest, New, *Hants.*
Freebridge Lynn, *Norf.*
Frome, *Som.*
Fulham, *London: Middx.*
Fylde, The, *Lancs.*

Gainsborough, *Lincs.*
Garrigill, *Cumbd.*
Garstang, *Lancs.*
Gateshead, *Dur.*
George, St., Blooms-
 bury, *London: Middx.*
George, St., Hanover
 Sq., *London: Middx.*
George, St., in the East,
 London: Middx.
George, St., Southwark,
 London: Surrey
Germans, St., *Corn.*
Giles, St., Bloomsbury,
 London: Middx.
Glandford Brigg, *Lincs.*
Glendale, *Nhmbd.*
Glossop, *Dbys.*
Gloucester, *Glos.*
Godstone, *Surrey*
Goole, *Yorks. W.R.*
Gower, *Glam.*
Grantham, *Lincs.*
Gravesend, *Kent*
Great Broughton, *Ches.*
Greenwich, *London:
 Kent*
Grimsby, *Lincs.*
Grinstead, East, *Sussex*
Guildford, *Surrey*
Guiltcross, *Norf.*
Guisborough, *Yorks.
 N.R.*

Hackney, *London:
 Middx.*
Hailsham, *Sussex*
Halifax, *Yorks. W.R.*
Halstead, *Essex*
Haltwhistle, *Nhmbd.*
Ham, West, *Essex*
Hambledon, *Surrey*
Hampstead, *London:
 Middx.*
Harborough, Market,
 Leics.
Hardingstone, *N'hants.*
Hartismere, *Suff.*
Hartlepool, *Dur.*
Hartney Wintney,
 Hants.
Haslingden, *Lancs.*
Hastings, *Sussex*
Hatfield, *Herts.*
Havant, *Hants.*
Haverfordwest, *Pembs.*
Hawarden, *Flints.*
Hay. *Brecons.*
Hayfield, *Dbys.*
Headington, *Oxon.*
Headley, *Hants.*
Helmsley, *Yorks. N.R.*

Helston, *Corn.*
Hemel Hempstead,
 Herts.
Hemsworth, *Yorks.
 W.R.*
Hendon, *Middx.*
Henley, *Oxon.*
Henstead, *Norf.*
Hereford, *Heref.*
Hertford, *Herts.*
Hexham, *Nhmbd.*
Highworth, *Wilts.*
Hinckley, *Leics.*
Hitchin, *Herts.*
Holbeach, *Lincs.*
Holbeck, *Yorks. W.R.*
Holborn, *London:
 Middx.*
Hollingbourn, *Kent*
Holsworthy, *Devon*
Holyhead, *Ang.*
Holywell, *Flints.*
Honiton, *Devon*
Hoo, *Kent*
Horncastle, *Lincs.*
Horsham, *Sussex*
Houghton le Spring,
 Dur.
Howden, *Yorks. E.R.*
Hoxne, *Suff.*
Huddersfield, *Yorks.
 W.R.*
Hull, *Yorks E.R.*
Hungerford, *Berks.*
Hunslet, *Yorks. W.R.*
Huntingdon, *Hunts.*
Hursley, *Hants.*

Ipswich, *Suff.*
Islington, *London:
 Middx.*
Ives, St., *Hunts.*

James, St., Westmin-
 ster, *London: Middx.*

Keighley, *Yorks. W.R.*
Kendal, *Westmd.*
Kensington, *London:
 Middx.*
Kettering, *N'hants.*
Keynsham,, *Som.*
Kidderminster, *Worcs.*
Kingsbridge, *Devon*
Kingsclere, *Hants.*
Kings Lynn, *Norf.*
Kings Norton, *Worcs.*
Kingston-on-Hull,
 Yorks. E.R.
Kingston-on-Thames,
 Surrey
Kington, *Heref.*

Kirkby Moorside, *Yorks.
 N.R.*
Knaresborough, *Yorks.
 W.R.*
Knighton, *Radnors.*

Lambeth, *London:
 Surrey*
Lampeter, *Cards.*
Lancaster, *Lancs.*
Lanchester, *Dur.*
Langport, *Som.*
Launceston, *Corn.*
Launditch, *Norf.*
Ledbury, *Heref.*
Leeds, *Yorks. W.R.*
Leek, *Staffs.*
Leicester, *Leics.*
Leigh, *Lancs.*
Leighton Buzzard,
 Beds.
Leominster, *Heref.*
Lewes, *Sussex*
Lewisham, *London:
 Kent*
Lexden, *Essex*
Leyburn, *Yorks. N.R.*
Lichfield, *Staffs.*
Lincoln, *Lincs.*
Linton, *Cambs,*
Liskeard, *Corn.*
Liverpool, *Lancs.*
Llandilo Fawr, *Carms.*
Llandovery, *Carms.*
Llanelly, *Carms.*
Llanfyllin, *Mont.*
Llanrwst, *Denbs.*
Loddon, *Norf.*
London, City, *London:
 Middx.*
London, East, *London:
 Middx.*
London, West, *London:
 Middx.*
Long Ashton, *Som.*
Lynn, Freebridge, *Norf.*
Lynn, Kings, *Norf.*

Macclesfield, *Ches.*
Machynlleth, *Mont.*
Madeley, *Salop.*
Maidenhead, *Berks.*
Maidstone, *Kent,*
Maldon, *Kent*
Malling, *Kent*
Malmesbury, *Wilts.*
Malton, *Yorks. N.R.*
Manchester, *Lancs.*
Manchester, South,
 Lancs.
Mansfield, *Notts.*

Margaret, St., Westminster, *London: Middx.*
Market Bosworth, *Leics.*
Market Harborough, *Leics.*
Marlborough, *Wilts.*
Martin, St., in the Fields, *London: Mdx.*
Martley, *Worcs.*
Marylebone, St., *London: Middx.*
Medway, *Kent*
Melksham, *Wilts.*
Melton Mowbray, *Leics.*
Mere, *Wilts.*
Meriden, *Warw.*
Merthyr Tydfil, *Glam.*
Middlesbrough, *Yorks. N.R.*
Midhurst, *Sussex*
Mildenhall, *Suff.*
Mile End Old Town, *London: Middx.*
Milton, *Kent*
Mitford, *Norfolk*
Molton, South, *Devon*
Monmouth, *Mon.*
Montgomery, *Mont.*
Morpeth, *Nhmbd.*
Mutford, *Suff.*

Nantwich, *Ches.*
Narberth, *Pembs.*
Neath, *Glam.*
Neots, St., *Hunts.*
Newark, *Notts.*
Newbury, *Berks.*
Newcastle in Emlyn, *Carms.*
Newcastle under Lyme, *Staffs.*
Newcastle on Tyne, *Nhmbd.*
Newent, *Glos.*
New Forest, *Hants.*
Newhaven, *Sussex*
Newington St. Mary, *London: Surrey*
Newmarket, *Cambs. and Suff.*
Newport, *Mon.*
Newport, *Salop.*
Newport Pagnell, *Bucks.*
Newton Abbot, *Devon*
Newtown, *Mont.*
Northallerton, *Yorks. N.R.*
Northampton, *N'hants.*
North Aylesford, *Kent*
North Bierley, *Yorks. W.R.*

Northleach, *Glos.*
Northwich, *Ches.*
North Witchford, *Cambs.*
Norton, Chipping, *Oxon.*
Norton, Kings, *Worcs.*
Norwich, *Norf.*
Nottingham, *Notts.*
Nuneaton, *Warw.*

Oakham, *Rutland*
Okehampton, *Devon*
Olave, St., *London: Surrey*
Oldham, *Lancs.*
Ongar, *Essex*
Ormskirk, *Lancs.*
Orsett, *Essex*
Oswestry, *Salop.*
Otley, *Yorks. W.R.*
Oundle, *N'hants.*
Ouseburn, Great, *Yorks. W.R.*
Oxford, *Oxon.*

Paddington, *London: Middx.*
Pancras, St., *London: Middx.*
Pateley Bridge, *Yorks. W.R.*
Patrington, *Yorks. E.R.*
Pembroke, *Pembs.*
Penistone, *Yorks. W.R.*
Penkridge, *Staffs.*
Penrith, *Cumbd.*
Penzance, *Corn.*
Pershore, *Worcs.*
Peterborough, *N'hants.*
Petersfield, *Hants.*
Petworth, *Sussex*
Pewsey, *Wilts.*
Pickering, *Yorks. N.R.*
Plomesgate, *Suff.*
Plymouth, *Devon*
Plympton St. Mary, *Devon*
Pocklington, *Yorks. E.R.*
Pontardewe, *Glam.*
Pontefract, *Yorks. W.R.*
Pontypool, *Mon.*
Pontypridd, *Glam.*
Pool, *Mont.*
Poole, *Dorset*
Poplar, *London: Middx.*
Portsea Island, *Hants.*
Portsmouth, *Hants.*
Potterspury, *N'hants.*
Prescot, *Lancs.*
Presteigne, *Radnors.*
Preston, *Lancs.*

Preston, East, *Sussex*
Preston, Great, *Yorks. W.R.*
Prestwich, *Lancs.*
Purbeck, *Dorset*
Pwllheli, *Caerns.*

Radford, *Notts.*
Ramsbury, *Berks.*
Reading, *Berks.*
Redruth, *Corn.*
Reeth, *Yorks. N.R.*
Reigate, *Surrey*
Retford, East, *Notts.*
Rhayader, *Radnors.*
Richmond, *Surrey*
Richmond, *Yorks. N.R.*
Ringwood, *Hants.*
Ripon, *Yorks. W.R.*
Risbridge, *Suff.*
Rochdale, *Lancs.*
Rochford, *Essex*
Romford, *Essex*
Romney Marsh, *Kent*
Romsey, *Hants.*
Ross, *Heref.*
Rothbury, *Nhmbd.*
Rotherham, *Yorks. W.R.*
Rotherhithe, *London: Surrey*
Royston, *Herts.*
Rugby, *Warw.*
Runcorn, *Ches.*
Ruthin, *Denbs.*
Rye, *Sussex*

Saddleworth, *Yorks. W.R.*
Saffron Walden, *Essex*
St. -- see under name of Saint
Salford, *Lancs.*
Salisbury, *Wilts.*
Samford, *Suff.*
Saviour, St. (Southwark), *London: Surrey*
Scarborough, *Yorks. N.R.*
Sculcoates, *Yorks. E.R.*
Sedbergh, *Yorks. W.R.*
Sedgefield, *Dur.*
Seisdon, *Staffs.*
Selby, *Yorks. W.R.*
Settle, *Yorks. W.R.*
Sevenoaks, *Kent*
Shaftesbury, *Dorset*
Shardlow, *Dbys.*
Sheffield, *Yorks. W.R.*
Sheppey, *Kent*
Shepton Mallet, *Som.*
Sherborne, *Dorset*

Shields, South, *Dur.*
Shifnal, *Salop.*
Shipston on Stour, *Warw.*
Shoreditch, *London: Middx.*
Shrewsbury, *Salop.*
Skipton, *Yorks. W.R.*
Skirlaugh, *Yorks. E.R.*
Sleaford, *Lincs.*
Smallburgh, *Norf.*
Solihull, *Warw.*
Southam, *Warw.*
Southampton, *Hants.*
South Manchester, *Lancs.*
South Molton, *Devon*
South Shields, *Dur.*
South Stoneham, *Hants.*
Southwark, *London: Surrey*
Southwell, *Notts.*
Spalding, *Lincs.*
Spilsby, *Lincs.*
Stafford, *Staffs.*
Staines, *Middx.*
Stamford, *Lincs.*
Stepney, *London: Middx.*
Steyning, *Sussex*
Stockbridge, *Hants.*
Stockport, *Ches.*
Stockton, *Dur.*
Stoke Damerel, *Devon*
Stokesley, *Yorks. N.R.*
Stoke on Trent, *Staffs.*
Stone, *Staffs.*
Stoneham, South, *Hants.*
Stonehouse, East, *Devon*
Stourbridge, *Worcs.*
Stow, *Suff.*
Stow on the Wold, *Glos.*
Strand, *London: Middx.*
Stratford on Avon, *Warw.*
Stratton, *Corn.*
Strood, *Kent*
Stroud, *Glos.*
Sturminster, *Dorset*
Sudbury, *Suff.*
Sunderland, *Dur.*
Sutton, *Sussex*
Swaffham, *Norf.*
Swansea, *Glam.*
Swindon, *Wilts.*

Tadcaster, *Yorks. W.R.*
Tamworth, *Staffs.*
Tarvin, *Ches.*

Taunton, *Som.*
Tavistock, *Devon*
Teesdale, *Dur.*
Tenbury, *Worcs.*
Tendring, *Essex*
Tenterden, *Kent*
Tetbury, *Glos.*
Tewkesbury, *Glos.*
Thakeham, *Sussex*
Thame, *Oxon.*
Thanet, Isle of, *Kent*
Thetford, *Norf.*
Thingoe, *Suff.*
Thirsk, *Yorks. N.R.*
Thomas, St., *Devon*
Thornbury, *Glos.*
Thorne, *Yorks. W.R.*
Thrapston, *N'hants.*
Ticehurst, *Sussex*
Tisbury, *Wilts.*
Tiverton, *Devon*
Todmorden, *Lancs.*
Tonbridge, *Kent*
Torrington, *Devon*
Totnes, *Devon*
Towcester, *N'hants.*
Toxteth Park, *Lancs.*
Tregaron, *Cards.*
Trowbridge, *Wilts.*
Truro, *Corn.*
Tunstead, *Norf.*
Tynemouth, *Nhmbd.*

Uckfield, *Sussex*
Ulverstone, *Lancs.*
Uppingham, *Rutland*
Upton on Severn,
  Worcs.
Uttoxeter, *Staffs.*
Uxbridge, *Middx.*

Wakefield, *Yorks. W.R.*
Wallingford, *Berks.*
Walsall, *Staffs.*
Walsingham, *Norf.*
Wandsworth, *London:*
  Surrey
Wangford, *Suff.*
Wantage, *Berks.*
Ward, East, *Westmd.*
Ward, West, *Westmd.*
Ware, *Herts.*
Wareham, *Dorset*
Warminster, *Wilts.*
Warrington, *Lancs.*
Warwick, *Warw.*
Watford, *Herts.*
Wayland, *Norf.*
Weardale, *Dur.*
Wellingborough,
  N'hants.
Wellington, *Salop.*
Wellington, *Som.*
Wells, *Som.*
Welshpool, *Mont.*
Welwyn, *Herts.*

Wem, *Salop.*
Weobley, *Heref.*
West Ashford, *Kent*
Westbourne, *Sussex*
West Bromwich, *Staffs.*
Westbury on Severn,
  Glos.
Westbury, *Wilts.*
West Derby, *Lancs.*
West Firle, *Sussex*
West Flegg, *Norf.*
West Ham, *Essex*
Westhampnett, *Sussex*
Westminster, *London:*
  Middx.
West Ward, *Westmd.*
Wetherby, *Yorks. W.R.*
Weymouth, *Dorset*
Wharfedale, *Yorks.*
  W.R.
Wheatenhurst, *Glos.*
Whitby, *Yorks. N.R.*
Whitchurch, *Hants.*
Whitchurch, *Salop.*
Whitechapel, *London:*
  Middx.
Whitehaven, *Cumbd.*
Whittlesey, *Cambs.*
Whorwelsdown, *Wilts.*
Wigan, *Lancs.*
Wight, Isle of, *Hants.*
Wigton or Wigtown,
  Cumbs.

Willesden, *Middx.*
Williton, *Som.*
Wilton, *Wilts.*
Wimborne, *Dorset*
Wincanton, *Som.*
Winchcombe, *Glos.*
Winchester, *Hants.*
Windsor, *Berks.*
Winslow, *Bucks.*
Winstree, *Essex*
Wirrall, *Ches.*
Wisbech, *Cambs.*
Witham, *Essex*
Witney, *Oxon.*
Woburn, *Beds.*
Wokingham, *Berks.*
Wolstanton, *Staffs.*
Wolverhampton, *Staffs.*
Woodbridge, *Suff.*
Woodstock, *Oxon.*
Woolwich, *London:*
  Kent
Wootton Bassett, *Wilts.*
Worcester, *Worcs.*
Worksop, *Notts.*
Wortley, *Yorks. W.R.*
Wrexham, *Denbs.*
Wycombe, *Bucks.*

Yarmouth, Great, *Norf.*
Yeovil, *Som.*
York, *Yorks. E.R.*